Algorithm Audit: Why, What, and How?

Seeking to increase the social awareness of citizens, institutions, and corporations with regard to the risks presented by the acritical use of algorithms in decision-making, this book explains the rationale and the methods of algorithm audit. Interdisciplinary in approach, it provides a systematic overview of the subject, supplying readers with clear definitions and practical tools for the audit of algorithms, while also taking account of the political, business, and vocational obstacles to the development of this new field. As such, it constitutes an essential resource for students and researchers across the social sciences and humanities, as well as for professionals and policymakers, with concerns about the social consequences of algorithmic decision-making.

Biagio Aragona is an Associate Professor of Sociology at the University of Naples Federico II, Italy.

Routledge Advances in Research Methods

Researching Ageing
Methodological Challenges and their Empirical Background
Edited by Maria Łuszczyńska

Diagramming the Social
Relational Method in Research
Russell Dudley-Smith and Natasha Whiteman

Participatory Case Study Work
Approaches, Authenticity and Application in Ageing Studies
Edited by Sion Williams and John Keady

Social Causation and Biographical Research
Philosophical, Theoretical and Methodological Arguments
Georgios Tsiolis and Michalis Christodoulou

Beyond Disciplinarity
Historical Evolutions of Research Epistemology
Catherine Hayes, John Fulton and Andrew Livingstone with Claire Todd,
Stephen Capper and Peter Smith

Concept Analysis in Nursing
A New Approach
John Paley

Algorithm Audit: Why, What, and How?
Biagio Aragona

For more information about this series, please visit: www.routledge.
com/Routledge-Advances-in-Research-Methods/book-series/RARM

Algorithm Audit: Why, What, and How?

Biagio Aragona

Routledge
Taylor & Francis Group

LONDON AND NEW YORK

First published 2022
by Routledge
2 Park Square, Milton Park, Abingdon, Oxon OX14 4RN

and by Routledge
605 Third Avenue, New York, NY 10158

*Routledge is an imprint of the Taylor & Francis Group,
an informa business*

British Library Cataloguing-in-Publication Data
A catalogue record for this book is available from the
British Library

Library of Congress Cataloging-in-Publication Data
A catalog record has been requested for this book

ISBN: 9780367530914 (hbk)
ISBN: 9780367530921 (pbk)
ISBN: 9781003080381 (ebk)

DOI: 10.4324/9781003080381

Typeset in Times NR MT Pro
by KnowledgeWorks Global Ltd.

To Giulia, Guglielmo, Siria and Sveva, for all the times I have answered "Excuse me, but I am working".

Contents

Acknowledgements

First and foremost, many thanks to Enrica Amaturo, for his guidance throughout my academic career, and the detailed readthrough and critique of the entire manuscript. I would like also to acknowledge Susan Halford for inspiring me to explore the applications of social research methods to algorithms and other data-intensive technologies. Cristiano Felaco was an essential sounding board and source of valuable materials.

The research conducted in writing this book was in part supported by the innovative projects' fund of the University of Naples Federico II, my home, the place where I grow up as both a scholar, and a person.

Introduction

It is not easy to introduce this book. There are so many examples of algorithms impacting our lives and societies that it is difficult to make a choice. Then, during my writing, in England, a further algorithm designed for the governance of education produced inequality by lowering the A-level results of nearly 36% of students who could not sit exams due to the coronavirus pandemic.

The algorithm was employed by the Office of Qualifications and Examinations Regulation (OFQUAL) – a non-ministerial government department that regulates qualifications, exams, and tests in England – to combat grade inflation and moderate the teacher-predicted grades for A level[1] and General Certificate of Secondary Education (GCSE) qualifications in 2020. The use of the algorithm was justified because examinations were cancelled as part of the response to the COVID-19 pandemic. Of course, as it always happens when trying to automate administrative processes, the OFQUAL algorithm was developed with the best intentions, ensuring that qualification standards were maintained and that the distribution of grades followed that in previous years.

For A-level students, their school had already included a predicted grade as part of the Universities and Colleges Admissions Service (UCAS) application reference, which operates the application process for British universities. The UCAS application was submitted by 15th of January 2020 (15th of October 2019 for Oxford, Cambridge and medicine), and the grades had been shared with the students.

According to the UCAS application, Mithusan Thiagarajah, one A-level student at the high school in Surbiton, was offered a place to study medicine at Caius College, Cambridge. No one in Mithushan's school had ever gone to Cambridge before, his success was not only making him proud but also his school.

The A-level grades were announced on 13th of August 2020. Nearly 36% were lower than the predicted grade (Persaud, 2020). Unfortunately, Mithushan, who had been expected to achieve four A*s by his teachers, also had his results downgraded to one A* and three As, not enough for Caius College. The college withdrew its offer.

What had happened?

OFQUAL's algorithm is based on the record of each examination centre in the subject being assessed. Students' grades at small schools or those taking minority subjects were computed differently than those of students at large schools. When in the examination centre students were over 15, the teacher-predicted grade (called "centre assessed grade" (CAG)) was standardised according to the series of the last three years results of the centre. When in the examination centre the students taking the test were under 15, CAGs were used without comparing with the historical data of the centres. As a result, students at small schools or who were taking minority subjects received grades higher than teacher predictions, while the opposite happened for students at large schools. The formula for standardising grades was actually copying the disparities that exist in the British education system. Small schools or minority subjects are typical of private schools, while large state schools have open access policies, and historically they have educated a large number of minority ethnic students and vulnerable students, who often have a lower grade distribution. Unfortunately, Mithusan and many other top students with his socio-demographic characteristics did not fit the time series of their examination centre.

The OFQUAL algorithm example is not isolated. Not only Britain, but many other countries are increasingly using software to automate education services (Williamson, 2016; Landri, 2018) with the hope of cutting costs and making processes more efficient. This not only saves time and money but it is also promoted as fair and objective because it removes humans from decisions – as the OFQUAL algorithm was intended to remove teachers from grades – and it is also said to prevent prejudices and corruption.

By chance, my interest in auditing algorithms began with another algorithm designed for education, when in 2016 the Italian Ministry of Education employed an automated system for assigning teacher positions for the 2016/2017 school year. The algorithm followed a series of criteria, some of these were agreed with teachers' representatives and unions. The algorithm was developed by Hewlett and Packard and Finmeccanica, two major providers of hardware and IT services for public administrations. The success of the algorithm was to decide the final destination of the teachers, considering the following: positions available, teacher preferences, teacher scores (education rating, special conditions such as family member with disabilities, professional mobility, etc.), and several contextual variables (i.e., positions available in the same school of provenience, school level, age, etc.). The algorithm was recursive in nature, it was applied again and again, until filling in all the positions available.

The results were shocking: thousands of teachers transferred hundreds of kilometres from their homes, compared to others with a lower score who were assigned to a position in the same province where they lived. Teachers from Apulia and Calabria had to move to the province of Milan, when they should have been assigned to their regions; teachers from Padua got positions in Tuscany, and quite astonishingly, two Calabrian teachers with their child with autism were assigned to a school in Prato, Tuscany (Zunino, 2019). As a result, there were thousands of lawsuits and appeals. If the algorithm was originally designed to protect teachers from external influences, thus producing an effective and "neutral" decision, it was instead evaluated as non-neutral by the Regional Administrative Court, whose judgements confirmed that the algorithm made unjustifiable decisions based on the criteria set out in the ministerial regulation no. 241/2016 that implemented the extraordinary recruitment plan. The technical expertise requested by the court and performed by the University of Tor Vergata in Rome defined the algorithm as follows: "confused, incomplete, pretentious …. built on input data organized and managed in the wrong way" (Salvucci et al., 2017, p. 12).

As for OFQUAL, the case had wide coverage in the media. For the first time, Italian public opinion was faced with "algorithmic governance" (Musiani, 2013), which is based on automated and autonomous processes of decision-making. It is a type of power that is not always transparent and linear both because the algorithms operate in a wider system of relationships in which different elements act simultaneously, and because side effects can occur due to the lack of human surveillance or, in contrast, to human errors in the writing of the code (Diakopoulos, 2016). Before we go deeply into this, let us step back, and let me try to explain what is meant by an algorithm.

Algorithms

The word "algorithm" comes from the name of ninth-century Persian mathematician Muḥammad ibn Mūsā al-Khwārizmī. The term emerged later in late medieval Europe when his texts were translated into Latin. These texts contained a series of calculations translated into mathematical formulas such as addition, subtraction, multiplication, and division (Goldschlager and Lister, 1986). For many years, the word "algorithm" remained an obscure term associated with a step-by-step method of performing written elementary arithmetic. This changed in the mid-twentieth century when the emerging field of computer science adopted it to refer to a set of instructions for solving a particular problem that could be implemented by a computer.

Any attempt to have a precise definition of algorithms has been thwarted by their evolution (Gurevich, 2011). Algorithms are multiple (Bucher, 2018), both because they have multiple definitions and multiple uses. From a purely technical point of view, algorithms are defined as a set of instructions to carry out certain activities (Sipser, 2006) or, more specifically, as a procedure governed by precise instructions and defined by a series of steps (Berlinski, 2000), as well as a way to describe a computational procedure in an abstract and formalised way (Dourish, 2016). Technically, an algorithm comes after the creation of a model, which is after having formalised the problem and defined the objectives in computational terms. Kowalski (1979) argues that the algorithm derives from the separation between logic and control: the logic component specifies the domain of knowledge to be used for formulating a solution to a certain problem. The control component determines the problem-solving strategy through which this knowledge is applied. In other words, the logic specifies at the theoretical level what must be done, while the control defines how it will be operationally done. It follows that the efficiency of an algorithm can be improved by modifying the control aspects, both by providing further steps and by including new data (inputs) to elaborate its logic structure. However, the translation of logic in control is not always straightforward. Some theoretical constructs can be expressed as algorithms in the form of mathematical equations, while, in more complex cases, it is first necessary to translate a problem into a series of instructions (pseudo-codes), which must then be encoded (Goffey, 2008). In this latter case, there is a double translation: a formalisation of the problem (logical plan) and a translation of this logic into a structured series of instructions and steps that determine the functioning of the algorithm itself (the control flow statements). As noted by Bucher, the "If …. Then" statement is the simplest of all control flow statements, which is used to tell a program to run a specific part of the code only if the condition is estimated to be 'true'. She concludes that "an algorithm essentially indicates *what* should happen *when*" (Bucher, 2018, p. 40).

A big difference must be traced between algorithms that are deterministic, which follow the same steps again and again, and algorithms that can "learn" over time, so-called machine learning. Machine learning algorithms group data by a set of features that are defined according to the same data, so programmers do not need to write all the control statements. They have the ambition to adjust initial features by learning from subsequent data. These kinds of algorithms are very dependent on the training datasets that are used to make the machine learn, sometimes ending up not matching the desired outputs. For this reason, one of the most common ways in which algorithms can learn is supervised learning, where programmers give the set of relevant information and the output desired, so that the algorithm can detect these in new data. Further evolution of machine learning is deep learning. Deep learning allows machines to work on tasks that are difficult to model, such as face recognition or voice generation (Bengio et al., 2017). Generating speech from text is an increasingly common task thanks to the popularity of software such as Apple's Siri, Microsoft's Cortana, Amazon Alexa, and the Google Assistant. Many new software for speech recognition (i.e., Wavenet, Tacotron, Deepvoice, Voiceloop) make use of deep learning. The algorithm of this type of software is fed with a training dataset of audio data, and it learns the characteristics of that audio. If the training set is made of voice sounds, the algorithm will learn all the possible features of those voices. The algorithm will be able to generate "non-existent but human language-like words in a smooth way with realistic sounding intonations" (van den Ord et al., 2016, p. 5). Speech recognition can operate ultra-detailed pattern-matching between a known voice and a new one to be used for forensic purposes (Napolitano, 2020). Artists, hackers, and media activists are also exploiting it to generate nonexistent voices, genderless voices (such as Meet Q: www.genderlessvoice.com) or "voice cloning" and deepfakes.

Algorithms are multiple not only because they have different logics and programming languages, but also because they do very different things. Recommendation algorithms play an essential role in the current online environment (Milano et al., 2020). They command how web search results are displayed, curate news feeds, and control job and dating platforms, among other things. Recommendation algorithms are implemented in social media platforms and structure our preferences by suggesting what song we should play next, what movie we would like, or what is the latest series that we would love. Today, many companies use big data to make highly relevant recommendations. The key to the success of recommendation algorithms is to operationalise at the best "similarity". When you must recommend something to a user, the most logical thing to do is to find people with "similar" interests, analyse their behaviour, and recommend that user the same items. You can also look at the items "similar" to ones that the user bought previously and recommend products that are like them. To perform this task, many algorithms can be employed, varying from collaborative filtering and its modification, to deep learning.

The goal of algorithmically controlled decision-making processes, or automated decision systems (ADS), as those presented in the introduction, is different. In this case, algorithms aim at finding the best decision for a given problem. ADS are procedural systems in which decisions are initially, partly, or fully delegated to a public entity or company, which in turn uses algorithms to perform an action. This delegation – not of the decision itself, but of the execution – involves a decision model and the algorithm that translates this model into computable code. Algorithmic decision systems are increasingly being used as part of decision-making processes with potentially significant consequences for individuals, organisations, and societies as a whole.

A long time before automation, algorithms took the form of ranking and classification systems. In education, algorithms have been employed to produce rankings of universities, schools, departments, professors, and students. These have a significant impact on student enrolments, research, and teaching funds. Another recent example of a ranking system is the algorithmic determination of risk conditions that has been employed during the COVID-19 pandemic to classify Italian regions, for example, into three categories (yellow, orange, and red) according to a set of indicators. The colour determined which actions citizens were allowed to perform, whether they could move between municipalities, go to restaurants, or visit relatives.

Algorithms are increasingly intertwined with culture and society. Therefore, several authors have started to dismiss a too simplistic technical definition of algorithm, in favour of a more complex one that recognises the crucial role that algorithms play in the social, political, and economic environments.

Beyond technicism

The expanding use of algorithms in society has called for the emergence of "critical algorithm studies" (Seaver, 2013; Gillespie, 2014) across several fields, ranging from media studies to geography and from sociology to the humanities. Inspired by science and technology studies (STS) literature about the blurring boundaries between technoscience and culture (Haraway, 1997), critical algorithm studies pay particular attention to the social and political consequences of outputs, such as how the algorithmic circulation of contents affects cultural consumption (Beer, 2013), how the massive use of algorithms has effects in markets and finance (Mackenzie, 2019), or how ADS centred on algorithms may reinforce inequalities and embed cultural biases (Noble, 2018; Espeland and Yung, 2019; Aragona, 2020). Within this emerging stream of studies, there is widespread agreement in considering the algorithm as a complex set of steps defined to produce specific results that intertwine social and material practices that have their own cultural, historical, and institutional nature (Takhteyev, 2012; Napoli, 2014; Dourish, 2016; Aragona and De Rosa, 2017). The objectivity, impartiality, and consequent claim of reliability of algorithms are contested: the same codes reflect the social and political values of their programmers. Even if they try to remain detached and impartial, they will bring their personal background of knowledge and their own thoughts and cultural models (Gillespie, 2014). Moreover, the design of an algorithm is also bound to the available resources and the quality of the data, by the set of requirements that regulate its use (standards, protocols, and laws in force), as well as by strictly technological instruments, such as platform, hardware, software, and infrastructure (Neyland, 2015; Diakopoulos, 2016). As such, algorithms are interpreted as part of much larger and more complex assemblages of actions and decisions, defined as "socio-technical systems composed of several apparatuses and elements that are deeply intertwined" (Kitchin and Lauriault, 2014, p. 6).

The term "assemblage", in French *agencement*, is attributed to the French philosopher Deleuze. He believed that assemblage is above all the attitude of recognising the production of technical elements as fields of force in the entity in which they are located and to which they contribute to produce (Deleuze and Guattari, 1980). In the assemblage, the technological stack – which includes hardware, codes, platforms, data, interfaces, etc. – and the forms of knowledge, the needs, and the interests of designers are inextricably entwined (Kitchin, 2017). Just as algorithms are a product of the assemblage, the assemblage is structured and managed to produce those algorithms (Ribes and Jackson, 2013). Algorithms and their assemblage are thus mutually constituted and, importantly, they are responsive, dynamic, and lively, and constantly reconfigured (Andrejevic, 2013). Gillespie (2014) uses the rhetorical figure of the synecdoche to effectively show the socio-technical nature of algorithms, seen as complex systems in which the algorithm itself, the reference models, the objectives, the data, and the programs, are connected and intertwined with the work of technicians and experts who discuss the models used, who are engaged in data processing and management, who design and apply algorithms in specific contexts. If algorithms are the combined product of different apparatuses, layered analytic techniques, and various competing communities of experts, their origins and interpretations become multiple and conflicting with the result of their assemblage being "black boxed".

"Black box" is a term used by cybernetics when a part of a mechanism or a series of instructions is unknown, apart from its inputs and outputs. We wonder, therefore, to what extent it is possible to access the operations carried out by algorithms that seem essentially opaque (Burrell, 2015), and how to reconstruct the complex of dynamics and interactions between the different actors (human and non-human) who co-participate in the construction of the algorithms. For this purpose, it becomes necessary to open the "black box" that governs them and break down the process in which they are designed and developed (Seaver, 2013). The opacity of algorithms has become a problem since they have been employed for normative purposes and for the management of public services. Algorithms play a crucial role in, for example, preventing and combatting crime in the context of predictive policing, or for supporting choices regarding hiring and firing in the workplace, and for selecting the audience of beneficiaries of welfare measures, not to mention the wide use in education policymaking and evaluation (Nakamura, 2013; Grosser, 2014; Aragona and De Rosa, 2017). When used appropriately, with due analysis of their impacts on people's lives, algorithmic systems, including artificial intelligence (AI) and machine learning, have been said to have great potential to improve human rights and democratic society. On the other hand, their opacity may raise disturbing questions on equity, democracy, and justice. Eubanks (2018), for example, shows that in the United States of America, many requests for health, food, or economic aid have been denied due to flawed computer systems, unreliable indices of distress, and invalid formulae. The adoption of data-intensive systems for selecting the audience of beneficiaries of welfare measures, which was supported by neoliberal logic as an antidote to inefficiency and waste, has in some cases had heavy consequences on the lives of the poorest citizens and socially excluded, especially African Americans. In one of the cases described by Eubanks in her volume regarding the allocation of beds to the homeless in the city of Los Angeles, the algorithm counted the nights spent in prison as housing, lowering the vulnerability index to those who were arrested, thus reducing their possibility to access in the future the few beds available (*ibid.*, p. 126).

As reported by the Panel for the Future of Science and Technology of the European Parliament in 2019 (Koene et al., 2019), there is growing concern that unless appropriate governance frameworks are put in place, the opacity of algorithmic systems could lead to situations where individuals are negatively impacted because "the computer says NO", with no recourse to meaningful explanation, a correction mechanism, or a way to ascertain faults that could bring about compensatory processes.

Very often the algorithms are opaque, unquestioned, and unaccountable (O'Neil, 2016). As in the case of the *Buona Scuola* algorithm, one aspect was particularly disapproved by the teachers: the not open nature of the algorithm and the difficulty to control it. When questioned about the evident errors, both the ministry and the software houses had at the first a protective behaviour, imputing the failure of the algorithm to the large amount of data to be treated. The same happened with the OFQUAL algorithm. The dispute began with comments made by the Royal Statistics Society in which the society said it had offered to help with the algorithm, but had objected to the proposed confidentiality agreement that experts would be required to sign, and claimed it had received no official response to its concerns. In principle, it is understandable that administrations defend the results of their algorithms. People impacted, domain experts, and technicians may all legitimately question the algorithms and their functioning, but from the point of view of administrations, the continuous contesting may raise uncertainty. Nevertheless, unquestioned and unaccountable algorithms may in the long term have worst effects on trust than control and scrutiny. The risk is that citizens will increasingly become suspicious about the use of algorithms, further fuelling doubts and distrust about their functioning in administration. To mitigate these legitimate fears, growing openness is needed, and this is where this book on algorithm audit starts.

Algorithm audit

An algorithm audit aims to promote two separate, but intertwined forms of openness: transparency and accountability. Transparency means that people impacted by an algorithm should be able to know what the algorithm does. If we cannot know what an organisation has delegated the algorithm to do, we cannot hold it accountable. Accountability means that people impacted by algorithms should be able to also know why administrations decide to design the algorithm as it is. Decision-makers should account for their decision in the first instance to use an algorithm to perform the task and solve technical as well as social and political choices that determined its final form. Transparency and accountability provide two important means to achieve algorithmic fairness. As mentioned earlier, algorithms may have the potential to automatically disadvantage, or even discriminate against, different social groups and demographics. Transparency and accountability minimise their potential to be unfair and maximise their potential to be fair. The assessment of fairness depends on evidence, events, and objectives, and therefore must be understood as situation or task-specific and necessarily addressed within the scope of practice by considering how case-specific activities and effects fit into broad social values.

Bucher (2018) underlines that the most common way to define an algorithm is to describe it as a recipe with its ingredients, their quantities, and the sequence of the steps to follow. The algorithm would be a set of instructions as those for how to bake a cake, make a risotto, or mix a Negroni cocktail. The problem is that the recipes of algorithms almost always cannot be found in any cookbook, but they are rather those kinds of recipes that a top chef (as well as my mum) will never tell you properly, sometimes because that recipe is protected by trade secrecy or intellectual property rights. We can push forward with the food metaphor, understanding the transparency of algorithms as the nutrition facts label that it is placed on every food product. Nutrition fact labels provide detailed information about the food's nutrient content, such as the amount of fat, sugar, salt, and proteins. They inform people about the differences in food nutritional capacities, calories, and ingredients. Nutrition information on food labels is regarded as a major means for encouraging consumers to make healthier choices when shopping for food (Baltas, 2001; Cheftel, 2005). The transparency of algorithms can have similar objectives. It can increase the awareness of citizens about algorithmic governance and automated data processing. Some (Kemper and Kolkman, 2019) consider transparency a utopia because the public cannot know; it does not have the right skills to understand algorithms. This is true today, just as, apart from rare cases, most of the people belonging to my father's generation did not know what saturated fats were and what effects high levels of sugar in blood could cause. After the Second World War in Europe, it did not make much sense to question the nutritional value of food because the important thing was just eating. After widespread levels of well-being have enriched our diets with elaborate, packaged, and industrial products, the consumption of meat has increased fivefold, and various types of sweets have invaded our tables, only then did we realise that it would have been appropriate to communicate with more clarity the nutritional values of the foods on the labels, giving ample visibility to the recipe (the black box). Today, we all know that diabetes can cause heart attacks and hypercholesterolemia may increase the odds of a stroke. Now not only nutritional values, but also critical production choices such as organic, palm oil free, no GMO, etc. are clearly communicated to consumers on the food packaging. Yes, it is true, most of the population does not know how algorithms work and what kind of problems they can generate. However, we ask for transparent algorithmic systems because they are becoming so central to our lives and economies, and we can imagine in 10/20 years a future where algorithms are receiving a colour according to their level of fairness, similar to how it happens on the new nutritional labels for food. I know that this may turn out to be difficult and controversial – also in the food market the colours have not been seen with favour – but that is just a provocative way to say that many efforts should be devoted to set algorithmic fairness standards, define best practices of transparency and accountability, and continuous benchmarking between similar algorithms.

To achieve this, the very first step is to gather and disseminate much evidence about algorithms and their functioning. I believe that social research methods may represent valuable tools for finding this evidence, and increasing transparency and accountability.

The first method is the experiment, a traditional method that may be used to test the algorithm with an equivalent dataset, or in different contexts, or to change a small part of the code to see what consequences it has on the results. A recent experiment conducted by Kayser-Bril (2020) showed that the algorithm used by Google Vision Cloud – an automatic image classification service – produced different results based on the colour of the skin. The image to be classified in the experiment was a hand holding a handheld thermometer, an object that before the recent new coronavirus epidemic was known only to specialists, but today it has become a common object, which individuals have seen on TV or in companies, airports, bus and train stations, and wherever it has become mandatory to measure temperatures. Google's automatic image classification system had been trained on datasets that probably did not contain images of handheld thermometers, so they could not classify the object correctly. Google Vision Cloud, however, was going to classify the object of a black individual holding the handheld thermometer as a "gun", while in the same image depicting a white individual, the object was classified as an "electronic instrument". The cause of this error is simple if you know how algorithms "learn" from data to make a classification of elements. The classification is made based on models that help the machine to interpret the image, so for example, cows that are photographed on a snowy mountain can be more easily classified as wolves, while, if they are in the city, as dogs. The context, in practice, can influence the classification. Kayser-Bril concluded that in the images used by Google to train the algorithm, black people were probably more frequent in violent scenes; therefore, the image of a black individual was more likely classified with a term that belongs to the lexicon of violence. The real consequences of such an obvious algorithmic bias can be severe. In the United States of America, automatic weapon recognition tools are used in schools, stadiums, and supermarkets. Likewise, in Europe, they are employed by some police forces in crowded places. As these systems are very similar to Google Vision Cloud, they may suffer from the same problem, making black individuals more likely to be considered dangerous. The Kayser-Bril experiment prompted Google on 6 April 2020 to modify its algorithm, and since then handheld thermometers have been classified correctly regardless of the colour of the skin of the person holding them.

Qualitative methods can also be very useful in auditing algorithms. Ethnography, for example, focuses on how algorithms are generated and how pre-analytical decisions on data and model preparation can affect results. It aims at understanding the symbolic, cultural, and normative values that are embedded in the algorithms, and which promote certain images of social reality. For example, Aragona and Felaco (2019) analysed some European data infrastructures and their network of stakeholders (administrators and policymakers, politicians, business companies, and others), showing that any of them has its own objectives that may be partly in conflict. The scholars report the case of the Italian Statistical Institute – one of the European Statistical Institutes that is exploiting the potential of big data for decision-making – that used detailed call records, processed with a complex spatial algorithm, to produce granular information on the population that insists for work or education in metropolitan areas. This is a part of a population that increases the presences in a given place, and its estimation is extremely helpful for organising public services and transports. In Italy, mobile phone companies are under no obligation to share data. Therefore, their use must be negotiated between the company and the institute, and it involves a layered of privacy authorities, governmental agencies, and private companies, and the signing of a series of agreements concerning intellectual property, non-disclosure, and re-sharing. In the case studied by the authors, it took two years to obtain an agreement and only with one of the three major companies working in the country. This may have consequences when comparing the results in different areas because of the number of clients in the different areas of the country. While this study did not highlight inequalities, it served to reaffirm the co-constitutive nature of algorithms, which is studded with actors, who sometimes must negotiate and reach a compromise, which has consequences for the algorithm.

Compromises, negotiations, all things that are not generally part of the narratives that promote the widespread adoption of ADS. These narratives instead insist on the efficiency, neutrality, and objectivity of the algorithms.

The range of techniques that can be useful for performing algorithm audits could continue (Chapter 3). For example, techniques include surveys of the stakeholders and on the population subject to algorithm, which aims to detect the behaviour and opinions of the people affected by specific automated decisions; or with participatory research for recruiting individuals who can act as users on APP and data-intensive systems and collect the results to be sent to researchers (Rogers, 2013). These are just to mention a few. In practice, there are now many strategies that can be followed to conduct research designs that have an algorithm as the object of study. In each of these, the role of an expert in social research methods (both quantitative and quali- tative, and digital/non digital) is crucial. Only empirical research can allow us to put aside prejudice and instead enter into the merits of the functioning of algorithmic systems. The more research is carried out, the more it will be possible to analyse the continuous feedback that exists between algorithms, knowledge, and decisions and assess their impact on ethics, inequality, and discrimination.

Note

1. The General Certificate of Education (GCE) Advanced Level, or A Level, is a main qualification for leaving school in England and other countries. Most students study three or four A-level subjects simulta- neously during the two post-age 16 years (ages 16–18) as part of their further education. A Levels are recognised by many universities as the standard for assessing the suitability of applicants for admission, and many such universities partly base their admissions offers on a student's predicted A-level grades, with the majority of these offers conditional on achieving a minimum set of final grades.

1 Why

Introduction

The rising need to audit algorithms can be seen as the latest sign of the process of datafication of governments and policymaking that began a long time ago (Espeland and Stevens, 1998). The link between data and politics is not new; indeed, statistics, from its very beginning, combined "the norms of the scientific world with those of the modern, rational state" (Desrosières, 1998, p. 8). At least since the foundation of the European nation states, knowledge in the form of data has represented an instrument of power. According to Hacking (1982), from 1820 to 1840, extraordinary and nearly universal numerical enthusiasm produced an avalanche of numbers, and techniques for their production, analysis, and communication. In the mid-twentieth century, Lasswell (1951) promoted a policy model where the improvement of policymaking relied upon a full scientisation of the policy process, and where data and related technologies played a crucial role. In his view, there was a single scientific truth that represented a certain policy problem, and through numbers and formulas the experts were able to fit this truth within the policy process. Once this truth was communicated to policymakers, then policies would be formulated around it. This view of data and related techniques has remained unchallenged for a long time, and it has been practised with only minor changes – for example, in the contexts of evidence-based policies (Davies et al., 2007) and in new public management (Lane, 2000), where the idea is "helps people make well informed decisions about policies, programmes and projects by putting the best available evidence from research at the heart of policy development and implementation" (Davies, 2012, p. 3). In order to achieve this evidence, the best experts in academia, IT services, and statistics should be employed, creating new forms of collaboration and exchange between public and private actors. This model

DOI: 10.4324/9781003080381-1

is considered key to enhancing efficiency and effectiveness, as well as reinforcing the legitimacy of political decisions, dismissing any form of ideology that could intervene in the design, and implementation of policies. The same discourses that justify datafication *mutatis mutandis* justify the implementation of algorithmic governance. Algorithms are employed to reaffirm political legitimacy and governmental authority, defending the logic of political decisions against ideology and sentiment, and promoting efficiency and effectiveness.

A rich field of study, starting in the 1980s and influenced by the works of Bourdieu (1979, 1988, 1991) on state and symbolic power, began to question this traditional objectivist and pragmatist vision of datafication. In such a new context, data were seen as the results of deliberate processes of choice, selection, and justification – in other words, as the outcome of a political process. Much research (Desrosières and Thévenot, 1988; Salais and Storper, 1993; Desrosières, 2010) has been devoted to studying the processes whereby classifications, indicators, and measures are constructed through a series of conflicts, compromises, and agreements between many actors with different cognitive frames. Common to these quite different studies is the notion, informed in part by the work of Foucault (1980), that administrative practices create what they intend to represent. Data then have a conventional nature or, in Thévenot's (1984) words, data become "agreed" within a specific format that is used in a particular action and justification regime. Hacking (2007) showed that scientific knowledge and experts participate in these political processes where facts and data are created, and they also become the main field where this political process is concretised. Indexes, indicators, registers, archives, and the related techniques for managing and analysing data and algorithms are just an outcome of the "'politics of indicators'" (Salais, 2004).

A further theoretical reference that can be extremely useful to critically unfold the intensive use of data and algorithms in public decision-making corresponds to three notions introduced by Amartya Sen. The first is the informational basis of judgement. Sen (1990) believed that any judgement is only based on specific data that inevitably exclude other kinds of data. According to the data selected, decision-making will follow some specific objectives and will make use of different instruments. The choice between alternative bases of judgements is therefore not the consequence of any scientific evidence, but is just politics. The second notion is the choice of the base of description. Sen explains that description is not merely a distant observation of a problem, but it implies the choice between different descriptions of the problem that are laden with theories and beliefs. But maybe the most important notion of the work of Sen is what he calls "positional objectivity" (1993), according to which, objectivity depends on the position of the observer. Observers are many and various (administrators and policymakers, politicians, corporations, researchers, journalists, citizens), and any of them has their own needs that may be partly in conflict. In contrast, algorithms are considered objective in an absolute sense, because they aim to be adopted in relation to different people and in many situations. Absolute objectivity means to refuse politics, seeing policymaking as simply a technical thing.

Technological determinism has also been attacked from a different perspective by science and technology studies (STS) (Latour, 1987), which have long been used to define data infrastructures (Star, 1999) and their importance in more recent works about the social life of data (Ruppert et al., 2015) or data assemblages (Kitchin and Lauriault, 2014; Aragona et al., 2018) that produce/reproduce new forms of digital data. Shifting from a matter of facts to a matter of concerns, STS allow us to focus on the heterogeneous assemblages in which meanings, descriptions, selections, codes, and choices are negotiated within a socio-material network of entities. Both computational and non-computational actions (Callon and Law, 2005) are performed in these assemblages, framing the object, the data, and the algorithms to collect and analyse the data. According to STS, data and related technologies do not exist prior to social action, but through social action (Bowker, 2013); nor do they exist independently of relational processes. Rather, they are the product of choices and constraints constituting systems of thought, technologies, people, resources and funding, knowhow, public and political opinion, and ethical considerations (Bowker and Star, 1999; Ribes and Jackson, 2013). Data and the algorithms that process them do not happen through unstructured social practices "but through structured and structuring fields, in and through which various agents and their interests generate forms of expertise, interpretation, concepts, and methods that collectively function as fields of power and knowledge" (Ruppert et al., 2017, p. 3). Inspired by STS, a growing number of scholars, in order to unpack the nature of algorithms, have started to focus critical attention on software codes and algorithms contributing to new media studies and software studies. Some have concentrated on how algorithms are generated (Geiger, 2017), others on how they work within a specific domain, such as journalism (Anderson, 2011), security (Amoore, 2006), or finance (Pasquale, 2015).

All these works show that algorithms, along with data, are not neutral. Far from being neutral in nature, algorithms construct and implement regimes of knowledge (Kushner, 2013), and their use has normative implications. The question, therefore, is whether this knowledge, the choices, the compromises, and the agreements are visible and publicly questionable, and whether the construction of algorithms can be audited or, on the contrary, these processes are completely black boxed.

The black box problem

The black box is a sketch that computer scientists use when part of a machine is too complex. Instead of explaining the complex instructions, they draw a black box to communicate that they do not need to know what is inside it, but just what signals enter (the input) and exit (the output). Pasquale (2015) notes that the term "black box" is a useful metaphor for algorithms, given its own dual meaning. It can refer to a recording device, like the data-monitoring systems in planes, trains, and cars, or it can mean a system whose workings are mysterious: we can observe its inputs and outputs, but we cannot tell how one becomes the other. In the digital society, we face these two meanings daily: tracked ever more thoroughly by firms and government, we have no certain idea of just how far much of this information can go, how and why it is manipulated, or its consequences. Latour (1987) explains that with black boxes, regardless of the controversies that have marked their creation, the complexity of their mechanisms, and the size of the networks of communities that keep them alive, only the input and output count. The black box helps smooth things; it makes ordinary transactions faster and more efficient (Pasquale, 2015) because it allows that a series of elaboration and exchange processes are just taken for granted.

Two features of black boxes are extremely relevant for understanding why we should audit algorithms. First of all, in black boxes, context and content are inextricably entwined. It is not possible to see the circumstantial events that produce a certain solution, or the network of human and non-human actors that participate in the assemblage of the box. Definitions, objects, and data are just taken for granted and unquestioned, assuming that everyone knows what the content is and that this content is detached from the context. Secondly, black boxes enable the accomplishment of routines, intended as flows that facilitate exchange within and between organisational actors, establishing a "recognizable pattern of interdependent actions" (Feldman and Pentland, 2008, p. 96).

A prime example of how content and context merge in black boxes, and how routines can become cages from which it is difficult to escape, is the controversy that originated in Italy during the second wave of the Sars-CoV-2 pandemic. Due to an error in the calculation of the number of people infected according to the algorithm that computed the risk of contagion in Italy, the region of Lombardy was classified "red" (high risk) for the week between 17 and 24 January 2021. Being classified as red meant that retail trade activities were suspended, with the exception of sales of food and basic necessities. Moreover, in a red area, it is forbidden to consume food and drinks inside restaurants and bars. For the whole region, the Lombardian federation of shop-keepers *Confeserercenti* estimated a loss of about 600 million Euros over the period concerned, and it considered starting a class action against whoever caused damage to the shopkeepers.

How was it possible that the calculated number of people infected was higher than the actual number and that the algorithm conse-quently recommended the wrong decision?

In order to answer this question, it is necessary to reconstruct the entire story behind this error, a story that is made up of choices between the different descriptions, the scientific evidence, and the relationships between interinstitutional working groups. Everything started with the regulation released on 12 October 2020 by the Italian Ministry of Health that first mentioned the long-term positive cases. The definition of a long-term positive case is one who, although no longer presenting symptoms, continue to test positive in the Sars-CoV-2 molecular test 21 days after the appearance of the first symp-toms. In this case, a person who has been asymptomatic for at least a week can interrupt the quarantine and be considered not to be contagious. This definition updated the criteria for the interruption of isolation. This change in the description of infected people took into account above all the evidence from a Chinese study published in *Nature Medicine* in April 2020 (He et al., 2020), which had been cited by the World Health Organization in June 2000. The authors of the study explained that the viral load is very high just before and in the first days after the beginning of symptoms. After that, it tends to decrease gradually until it is almost undetectable on day 21. At the same time that Lombardy was classified as red, this evidence was confirmed by another article published in *The Lancet Public Health* (Quilty et al., 2021). Apparently, according to what was reported by the Italian National Institute of Health (ISS), it would seem instead that in all the data compiled weekly by the Lombardy region between October 2020 and January 2021, the long-term positive cases appeared as people with onset symptoms but without a description of their clinical status (asymptomatic, paucisymptomatic, etc.). Therefore, they were all registered by the algorithm as infected, even if in reality many of them had been asymptomatic for more than a week.

In the technical appendix that the Lombardy region sent to the Administrative Court on 20 January 2021, the Lombardy Region Health Department underlined that until then the overestimation had been masked by the significant increase in cases in the second wave (over 300,000). For this reason, the consequences of this miscalculation were noticed only at the end of January. To estimate how the choice of this new description impacted the calculation of infections, we can consider, for example, that by eliminating the cases for which an indication of asymptomatic clinical status was given where previously it was absent, in the week between 15 and 30 December 2020 the number of infections drastically reduced from 14,180 cases to only 4,918 (Capra, 2021). On 23 January 2021, the governor of Lombardy, Attilio Fontana, told the press that the region had not made a mistake. At the request of the reporters, he argued that the algorithm used by the ISS could be wrong. The ISS reacted immediately by claiming that the algorithm was correct and worked in the same way for all regions, reiterating that it was Lombardy that had made the mistake. Only the judicial authority will ascertain who is really responsible for this further economic loss and who will have to compensate the shopkeepers for this miscalculation that incorrectly inhibited their business activities.

This example clearly brings out all the characteristics of black boxes and their limitations. First of all, the transmission of data by the Lombardy region to the ISS was based on routines that were carried out thanks to the black box, wherein a lot is taken for granted. The routine flows of weekly data reports which facilitated exchanges between organisational actors and handled timely data during the previous seven months of the pandemic became a repeated loop performed in an acritical and somehow ritualistic way. Furthermore, the description of the number of infections, something that is wrongly perceived as objective and taken for granted, was not questioned even when the parameters of the calculation changed because of the incorporation of further scientific discoveries related to the spread of the infection. For about three months the problem was not noticed by either the ISS or the region, and they continued with the same routines. This happened because it is assumed that the description of the number of infections is the output of an independent technical evaluation and not the result of scientific and political choices. The consequences of the decision taken through the algorithm were uncontested until the controversies emerged. Paraphrasing Latour, we could say that this example clearly shows the two faces of algorithms, algorithms under construction and algorithms ready for use, as different as the two-faced Janus. The algorithm that calculated the spread of contagion, that seemed so sure, objective, and unquestioned – indeed, black boxed – has become instead a negotiable object, which puts work groups in competition with each other, which generates disputes, including legal ones, and which reveals its contextuality and accidental, unequal impact.

Latour (1987) explains that to discard black boxes you have to enter the service door, the one that brings you to the science under construction; but as we will see in Chapter 3, analysis of the algorithms in use can also be important in raising controversies that require the black boxes to be unpacked.

It is noted that blackness is not always an essential feature of algorithms. In principle, the algorithm that calculated the risk of contagion for the Italian regions was absolutely white. It has been described in detail, both in its calculation and in the description of the 21 indicators that constitute its input (Cori et al., 2013). But this did not prevent it from having the characteristics of black boxes (routines, taken for granted, unquestioned descriptions, etc.). Therefore, Bucher (2017) argues that rather than struggling with the fact that algorithms are boxes, and that they are black, we should adopt a conceptualisation of algorithms in terms of relational ontology, shifting from asking what algorithms are to what algorithms actually do. What remains is that thousands of people lost money because the decisions that were made through the algorithm impacted on their lives, while not impacting on the lives of other workers with different characteristics, and this is what really matters.

Digital social inequality

To clarify what is meant by digital social inequality, it is necessary to introduce a distinction between three terms that are sometimes used interchangeably: diversity, differences, and inequalities. At the origin, there is diversity between one individual and the next. We are all diverse from each other, not only from a physical and biological point of view, but also in terms of other types of ascribed features: the place where we were born, the family we come from, the social and natural environment that we find coming into the world. However, diversity is also acquired through experiences, notions, knowledge, skills, and culture. But diversity is not enough to create inequality: a process is needed to transform some diversities into socially significant differences – that is, into recognisable and identifiable differences in the light of the socio-cultural models prevailing in a certain society at a given historical moment. If differences become criteria for the distribution of collective resources, both in material and symbolic terms, then they produce inequalities. The distribution criteria are established on the basis, for example, of the division of labour, or by the structures of power that are legitimised on a symbolic and ideological level. Thus, inequality refers to the uneven distribution of collective resources (material and symbolic) in society, which is determined by the structures of power and the economy, as well as by symbolic universes and social representations, and, increasingly, by technology.

The example presented earlier on the shutting of shops in Lombardy demonstrates how an acquired diversity (having a certain job) is transformed by a socio-cultural model into a socially shared difference. More specifically, the shared difference in this case is the Nomenclature of Economic Activities (NACE), which groups organisations according to their business activities, an instrument that is almost globally employed to compare similar economic activities. NACE was the criterion upon which the decision to shut shops was made. The algorithm used to implement the criterion can contribute to accelerate the effects of inequalities and to automate them, as wisely documented in the riveting book by Virginia Eubanks (2018). Eubanks explains that automated decision-making can in the long term shatter the social safety net and intensify discrimination, because the individuals impacted by the decisions are targeted as members of social groups, not as individuals.

The analysis of the link between technology and inequality has been conducted from different perspectives. The first set of arguments takes up the question of the diverse use of technologies by social groups with different education, age, class, gender, and ethnicity. In line with the literature on the digital divide (Compaine, 2001; Norris, 2001), it is argued that disadvantaged groups are less likely to access broadband and digital technologies; they therefore develop fewer skills and are at the same time less aware of the risks of technology.

The early literature on the digital divide has been criticised for its tendency to separate the social from the technological, underestimating that it is in the crossroads between social disadvantage and poor access to technologies that digital social inequalities can nestle (Halford and Savage, 2010). The term "digital social inequalities" has the merit of affirming the bidirectional nature of the relationship between social disadvantage and lack of access to technologies, which has always been considered one-way. It is not simply the social dis-advantage that leads to limited access, but structural social factors and the use of digital technologies mutually configure one another, they co-constitute (Lupton, 2015). When social disadvantages, insufficient digital literacy, poor coding knowledge, and limited access to technology and the internet are intertwined, individuals may be more likely, on the one hand, to underestimate the risks of automated decision-making systems and, on the other, to have little trust in algorithmic technologies.

But how can algorithms generate or amplify social inequalities? Airoldi (2020), starting from a review of the literature on the subject, points out the way in which the algorithms implemented in search engines and in various online platforms tend to propose the most popular content (Broussard, 2018). The algorithms have an algorithmic authority (Rogers, 2013) to influence which sources are considered most important and relevant. This is the logic implemented in the Google search engine, for example, in platforms like YouTube, and in virtual assistants like Siri and Alexa. However, the heavier social consequences of the spread of the algorithmic culture (Hallinan and Striphas, 2016) occur when algorithms are used for regulatory purposes and for the management of public services. In fact, automated decision-making systems are used more and more often in public administration, sometimes with excellent results, sometimes with not exactly encouraging results, raising disturbing questions as to the level of equity.

Digital social inequality focuses on the link between social disadvantage and lack of digital and data literacy. Scarce knowledge of coding and data science, as well as limited access to technology and the internet, may result in a lack of ability to understand the risks of algorithmic decision-making. This lack is strongly related to gender, age, race, and class, as many research examples have shown. Recently, van Dijk (2020) collected 25 years of research in this field to address three often stated assumptions about the relationship between information communication technologies (ICT) and inequalities (ICT reduces social inequality; ICT makes no difference; ICT increases social inequality). In balancing the evidence, she ultimately states that digital inequality today not only reflects but also tends to reinforce social inequality. From a different perspective, Noble (2018) talks of technological redlining – that is, the perpetuation of racial, cultural, and economic inequities in technologies. The concept of redlining stems from a history of housing discrimination since the 1930s, where red lines were literally drawn on maps to segregate poor and dominantly black neighbourhoods. Today, redlining is concretised in automated decisions based on race, gender, and geography. The cause of technological redlining is pinpointed in the asymmetry of power between the creators of ICT and those who are more impacted by them, the most disadvantaged people. Nguyen (2019) concludes that to address digital social exclusion, tech companies should calibrate their hiring process to ensure more inclusion of people of colour, women, etc. In contrast, white men dominate the IT roles and college computer departments. Without diversity in computer education, it will not be possible to reduce technological redlining.

Things get even more problematic with public bodies' increasing implementation of digital technology in order to automate decision systems and eligibility for services and policies. According to the EU parliament, European citizens should become aware of algorithmic governance and automated data processing, otherwise the digital social inequalities will ultimately undermine the sense of trust in public administration and governments (Koene et al., 2019). As Noble (2018) foresees, artificial intelligence will become a major human rights issue in the twenty-first century.

Transparency and accountability of public bodies

The need to audit algorithms is in line with a progressive movement that has advocated that citizens should have the right to access documents and the proceedings of governments to allow effective public oversight. The United Nations sustainable development goals, for example, encourage public access to information as a criterion for ensuring accountable and inclusive institutions. The request for public access is the result of the increasing importance that transparency and accountability – the obligation for a subject to be responsible for its decisions and for the results achieved – are gaining in these times. Algorithmic transparency has been discussed at the professional, governmental, and activist levels – for example, within the Association for Computing Machinery, the White House, and the European Parliament. Transparency has a two-fold objective, cognitive and normative. On the one hand, it aims to return information to technicians and policymakers in order to redirect and improve political action; on the other hand, it allows citizens to know whether or not the policies implemented have had the expected effects.

Algorithmic transparency may be practiced by institutions in two main ways. First of all, an institution may become transparent by moving from black to white box, so that not only are inputs and outputs known, but also how the institution works internally. This kind of transparency originated long ago in European nation states when philosophers debated the construction of a democratic state, but it has become a focus in contemporary politics due to the opportunities opened up by ICT. Transparency is linked to the idea of open government. The European Union launched the *Open Government Partnership* in 2011, an initiative for openness, transparency, and civic participation which now sees the involvement of 78 governments that are committed to activating an open action plan in five thematic areas: participation, transparency, integrity, accountability, and technological innovation. The contemporary view of open government finds its strongest advocates in non-governmental organisations, which argue that standards of openness are vital to the enduring success and advance of democratic societies. Floridi (2014) stresses that there is also another innovative sense of transparency: this is when the technology is transparent not because is white, but "because it delivers its services so efficiently, effectively, and reliably that its presence is imperceptible …. one may speak of Gentle Governments" (pp. 188–189).

The limitations of transparency have been debated. If openness may represent the first answer to algorithmic opacity (Goodman and Flaxman, 2017), this will not automatically lead to transparency if that information is not understood by the relevant audience. As noted before, the impact of algorithms should not be estimated without unfolding how they become embedded in the networks of people and existing systems that make use of them. Algorithms cannot be separated from the practices in which they are designed, programmed, and used (Geiger, 2017). Measures towards algorithmic accountability are thus most effective if we consider them a property of socio-technical assemblages of people and machines (Kemper and Kolkman, 2019). There is therefore a growing need for studies that assess the conditions in which measures of transparency actually yield positive effects by fostering a productive relationship with an audience. In contrast, many theorisations of transparency are a priori considered as emancipatory, revelatory, and empowering, without reference to the target. Kemper and Kolkman (2019) explain that we should ask: transparent to whom? Transparency must be understood as meaningful for a given target in order for any (critical) engagement to emerge (Betancourt, 2017). For this reason, transparency is not the ultimate answer to algorithmic opacity. Other measures should be developed to educate a critical audience of citizens and relevant decision-makers and disseminate knowledge about algorithms. One key to transparency is indeed algorithmic awareness – that is, the extent to which citizens and other individual and collective social actors are conscious of being objects and subjects of algorithmic authority. First of all, people should become aware of being data producers and data owners, and of their (limited) ability to manage/use/protect data. Furthermore, they should increase their awareness of being increasingly ruled by algorithmic decision systems and algorithmic scores. In a context of data-intensive societies, algorithmic awareness is an important means to promote social inclusion. Only through this kind of awareness would it be possible to construct meaningful transparency, and the risk is that transparency is useless if there is no critical engagement. It is time to promote a path towards the understanding, interpretation, and evaluation of algorithmic-driven decisions and algorithmic-based arguments for all citizens.

In order to improve awareness of algorithmic authority, the European Parliament's Panel for the Future of Science and Technology suggested developing multidisciplinary and interdisciplinary research (Koene et al., 2019). Philosophers and experts in ethics, AI, computer science, social science, and law should work together to develop further understanding of the issues raised by algorithmic decision-making. More specifically, to develop an audience for transparency experts should join forces to understand the types of accounts and explanations that are most useful depending on the targeted audiences and their needs. Further progress also has to be made on the implementation of transparency by design. The experts of the Panel contended that a key condition to facilitating research is the possibility for scholars to obtain access, under specific conditions and strict confidentiality, to datasets. However, there are several limitations to the transparency of datasets. First of all, publicising a dataset may mean a loss of privacy. Furthermore, data-intensive technologies usually have copyrights and patents, so full disclosure may never be obtained. Last but not least, a lack of data literacy limits the ability of citizens and users to express agency in their interaction with these algorithmic systems, with the unintended consequence of undermining the pressure on the state and the market to regulate the sector. Ways to increase the awareness of citizens and social groups about data, algorithms, and the power that is exerted by them should be fully developed through long-lasting education programmes. Activists often press for transparency as a solution to the black box issue, but transparency may simply provoke complexity that obscures the understanding of people not really accustomed to algorithmic logic and who are not adequately data literate.

The lack of trust

If there is a risk that algorithmic processes may have unjust outcomes, this undermines citizens' feelings of security and trust in the processes themselves and in the institutions that use them. Chignard (2013) noted that the actors who are most determined to be transparent are also those most concerned by the crisis of trust that is affecting society: politicians, public institutions, companies involved in energy, transport, credit, the environment, etc. In practice, transparency is perceived as a response to the mistrust and distrust that citizens have towards certain companies and institutions, and their representatives.

One reason for this mistrust is the dystopian fear that machines will replace men in decisions. This belief is supported by those who think that machines make decisions; instead, it should be stressed that algorithms do not make decisions, they are just delegated to make decisions for agents that are responsible for the decisions made. Human intervention in algorithmic processes is high, and the algorithm fabric has a human weft: there are no unsupervised algorithms; rather, there are people who decide whether or not a certain threshold is acceptable, or what data source is to be used in a specific situation (Seaver, 2018). Human intervention has recently been strategically emphasised to prevent the dehumanisation of automated decision-making. Examples are the use of supervised learning instead of unsupervised machine learning, or the transition from AI to so-called human AI, which is artificial intelligence centred on people.

The second element of mistrust is that the extensive use of algorithms would lead to a form of technocratic government in which the role of ICT would be decisive (Lyon, 2017). An example of a technocratic process that is often cited by critics of algorithms is anticipatory governance, a form of profiling that is used to predict future behaviour and guide the interventions to be carried out (Kitchin and Lauriault, 2014). This form of profiling is very popular for regulating police inspections and checks – for example, at airports, where algorithms classify passengers by various levels of danger, with the result that they receive different treatment based on what they may or may not do (Amoore, 2006). A further example is the analysis of online traces, sensors, and the Internet of Things in urban contexts and in smart cities, which is said to generate Big Brother effects in which the pervasiveness of technology become a tool for control. These criticisms have been fostered by the suspicions raised by journalists and whistleblowers about the use of algorithms to control citizens. According to whistleblower Snowden (Greenwald, 2013), for example, through

PRISM, a surveillance program that began in 2007 in the wake of the passage of the Protect America Act under the Bush Administration, the National Security Authority (NSA) collected and algorithmically processed mass data far greater than the public knew. US government officials have disputed criticism of PRISM and have defended the program. However, the declarations by Snowden and other whistleblowers raised some ethical and political doubts about algorithms and their governmental use.

A further source of mistrust that is evoked to prevent algorithmic authority is that big data, data infrastructures, and related technologies to manage and analyse data, along with algorithmic systems, could accelerate the privatisation of the public sphere, because these types of activity are ruled by the main software and hardware companies and come from the major communication and logistics corporations.

Although we cannot fully agree with these criticisms, for automated algorithmic systems to be really effective not only in the short but also in the medium to long term, it is necessary to think about ways to foster trust. One way to build trust in algorithmic systems is seen in what some consulting firms are trying to construct around technology-packed government solutions. With the city of Amsterdam, for example, KPMG, together with the critical algorithm scholar Cathy O'Neil, are putting forward solutions to monitor algorithmic solutions and their performance by, on one side, detecting the ability to organise control of the adoption of automated solutions effectively and, on the other side, analysing the impacts that these systems have on organisations. These proactive control solutions, implemented by public and private partnerships under the surveillance of third-party bodies, which see an important role for researchers, can really be the most effective ways to foster trust in automated decision-making systems. These solutions anticipate the risks of algorithmic governance and are more successful in building trust than what is simply referred to as transparency, which, without an effective audience, leads nowhere.

Conclusions

This chapter aimed to demonstrate that the success of the application of algorithms in public administration will depend on the ability to produce empirical evidence regarding their quality, their functioning in society, and their risk of generating inequalities. An algorithm is not good or bad *per se*. Therefore, the position that should be taken with respect to the adoption of algorithmic procedures in the management of public services is an intermediate position, which is critical with respect to the indiscriminate and uncontrolled use of algorithms, but which, at the same time, welcomes the conscious and transparent use of automated decisions. Being aware does not mean hindering the spread of data-intensive decision-making systems; on the contrary, in the long run, it allows them to improve their work. It is only through careful examination of the pros and cons based on research results that algorithmic systems can be consciously adopted. The algorithm audit is the pivotal tool to monitor algorithmic authority; otherwise the risk is that algorithmic governance will continue to guide our lives without our intervention, and to produce new, and increasingly complex, forms of social inequality.

2 What

Introduction

The word "audit" derives from the Latin word *audire*, which means "to hear". Audit has been adopted since ancient times and extended to cover many fields, first in the private and then in the public sectors. The term is most frequently employed to audit the financial statements relating to a legal person. Audits can provide independent third-party guarantee to financial markets and other stakeholders that the business of a legal person is ethically run. The professional figure who has the competence to carry out an audit is called an auditor. The terms "audit" and "auditor" are heavily codified and have different meanings (in definite rules and regulations) according to the specific audit type. The introduction of quality assurance standards (e.g., International Organisation for Standardisation [ISO]) made the concept of audit widespread and practised. For example, the ISO management system standards define an audit as a systematic, independent, and documented process for obtaining evidence and evaluating it objectively. The audit can have different objectives, such as:

- To verify the degree of conformity with respect to a standard or a procedure
- To qualify a provider
- To issue a certificate of conformity
- To evaluate the effectiveness of corrective actions undertaken
- To verify and monitor services
- To acquire information on the degree of competence and awareness of people
- To achieve a rating (or a ranking) with respect to a scale that measures a certain performance

DOI: 10.4324/9781003080381-2

The need for auditing companies and organisations arose because their internal operations, like algorithms, look like black boxes to those on the outside. Independent auditors should then provide reasonable assurance that what comes from the black box is free of misstatement. The same logic applies to algorithms. In recent years, the need to audit algorithmic decision systems, AI, and, in general, all governmental applications of data-intensive technologies have been discussed at various levels by academics, NGOs, and governments. Several guidelines have been proposed worldwide. In North America, for example, there is the Institute of Electrical and Electronics Engineers (IEEE), which proposed the *Ethically Aligned Design*, and Canada's federal government passed the *Directive on Automated Decision-Making*, with the goal of supporting transparency and public accountability around the adoption of automated decision-making technologies. In Europe, the EU has approved its *Ethics Guidelines for Trustworthy AI*, and the European Parliament is discussing a governance framework for algorithmic accountability and transparency. The *General Data Protection Regulation* (GDPR) already requires that EU organisations be able to explain their algorithmic decisions. *Amnesty International UK* has also published its five overarching principles for an AI code. In Asia, Singapore declared its *Model Artificial Intelligence Governance Framework*, and Taiwan adopted the *Guidelines for the Research and Development of AI*. Japan's Ministry of Internal Affairs and Communication drafted its AI principles, besides other ethics guidelines designed by the Japan Deep Learning Association (JDLA) and Tokyo University. Some principles focus on algorithm design, whereas others are more about its usage and impacts on stakeholders. Some guidelines start from European ideologies, and some were offered from Asian standpoints. While in total more than 115 principles have been proposed (Hung and Yen, 2020), they roughly converge around a few aspects. First of all, algorithms should be accessible and explainable, and they should fit into the mechanisms of governments' accountability. Furthermore, data quality and security have to be a major concern, and data should be under proper protection over their entire cycle (from the input to the output). All guidelines and frameworks also acknowledge that algorithms may have negative impacts, especially on vulnerable groups (e.g., the poor and ethnic minorities), and the urgency that governments should handle them fairly. Finally, it is always stressed that the development and deployment of algorithmic governance aim to improve human well-being, citizens' rights, democracy, sustainable development, and security.

How can we produce scrutable evidence that all this is accomplished? For sure, an open-minded standpoint should be employed, where computer science, data science, and machine learning methods are needed, but surely not sufficient, for the foundations of an algorithm auditing discipline. Algorithm audit is interdisciplinary in nature and should integrate critical thinking, professional expertise, communication skills, and the use of scientific method. If computer scientists have to put their efforts into optimising the model to find patterns in data, it is the social scientist who may ask more critical questions about the quality and the relevance of those data for the objectives of the model. Other important questions are: Is the algorithm sufficiently transparent to targets? Does it pursue tolerable social values? Is there evidence of internal bias or incompetence in its design? Does it adequately explain how it arrives at a decision? How does it impact the institution that adopted it? These broader sets of questions should be encompassed in the audit of algorithms, moving the adoption of algorithms from being just a technical challenge to becoming a governmental and societal challenge. To illustrate what all this means, consider the use of algorithms in predictive policing. Predictive policing is based on the assumptions that certain aspects of the physical and social environment encourage predictable acts of criminal wrongdoing. Predictive policing aims to "forecast where and when the next crime will take place" (Uchida, 2014, p. 3871). The targeted units of predictive policing can go from different territorial or governmental areas to a singular individual and may be roughly classified into three types (Hung and Yen, 2020). Area-based policing targets the place in which wrongdoings are more likely to occur. Event-based policing targets the crime that is more likely to occur. Person-based policing targets the individual who is more likely to be involved in criminalities. Among these, person-based predictive policing is the most controversial, as it singles out individuals and assesses their risk according to personal features (Ferguson, 2017). A famous case of predictive policing that has caused many concerns is the Correctional Offender Management Profiling for Alternative Sanctions (COMPAS). This is an algorithmic decision tool developed and owned by Northpointe and employed by US courts in many states to assess the likelihood of a defendant becoming a recidivist. A first general critique of the use of proprietary software such as COMPAS is that, since the algorithms it uses are trade secrets, they cannot be examined by the public. Furthermore, the fairness of this tool is questioned, because it may exacerbate inequalities. Additionally, its design may pose selection biases where particular features have disturbing effects on the outcomes, and its implementation hugely impacts the institutions that adopt it. Having access to 7,000 risk scores assigned to people arrested in Broward County,

Florida, in 2013 and 2014, an investigation of *Propublica*[1] controlled how many defendants were charged with new crimes over the next two years, the same benchmark used by the designers of the algorithm. The *Propublica* team found that black defendants were almost twice as likely as whites to be labelled a higher risk of recidivism but not actually reoffend, whereas white defendants were much more likely than blacks to be labelled lower risk but went on to commit other crimes. The calculation of the risk score is derived from 137 questions that are either answered by defendants or pulled from criminal records. Race is not a question, but the algorithm considers education levels and whether a defendant has a job. COMPAS software is among the most widely used assessment tools in the United States. Northpointe does not publicly disclose the calculations used to arrive at defendants' risk scores, so either defendants or the public cannot scrutinise the algorithm. Defendants rarely have an opportunity to challenge their assessments. The results are usually shared with the defendant's attorney, but the calculations that transformed the underlying data into a score are rarely revealed. As often happens with risk-assessment tools, many jurisdictions have adopted the software, and judges are given defendants' Northpointe assessments during sentencing to ease and speed up their work. The COMPAS software is cited as an example of algorithmic inequality because the different false positive rates spotted by the *Propublica* team suggested racial bias. But Northpointe argued that the algorithm is not unequal, because the reoffending rate is approximately the same regardless of the defendant's race; a high score means approximately the same probability of reoffending (Dieterich et al., 2016). By changing the point of reference for evaluating inequality, the recidivism algorithm demonstrated fairness.

Although predictive policing remains a controversial and disputed example of algorithmic governance, these results show that algorithmic equality is far from uncontested. They also show that algorithm audit requires the operational definition of terms such as quality, fairness, and impact: "Algorithm audit must be intended as a scientifically grounded evaluation that is ethically informed by the conventions deliberated and established at the societal and governmental level" (Guszcza et al., 2018). Algorithm audit is an important part of the broader challenge of creating reliable algorithmic decision systems and defining and implementing standards for the development and deployment of algorithms in the public sphere. To define more precisely what algorithm audit is, we must refer to the four main elements upon which the expert evaluation should be expressed: the data, the model, the fairness, and the impact. It is by evaluating and assessing these four elements that algorithms can more and more reflect shared societal values.

The data

The data inputted in algorithms should be of the best quality. Unfortunately, data quality is not absolute, the quality of data is composed of many dimensions, and data quality often should be evaluated by considering the different trade-offs between its components. According to the main definitions adopted by international statistical offices such as Eurostat (2009) and the OECD, there are at least five main dimensions of data quality: accuracy, timeliness, comparability, relevance, and accessibility.

Accuracy

When one thinks of data quality, often one thinks of accuracy. Accuracy is the degree of closeness of computations or estimates to the exact or true values that the data were intended to measure. The concept of accuracy is further broken down into selection and non-selection error. The difference between a population value and an estimate derived from a selection from that population is a selection error. One example of selection errors is coverage errors. A coverage error occurs when the target population does not coincide with the available population (Mulry, 2008) because of undercoverage and overcoverage. For example, the calculation of the risk of contagion from COVID-19 in Lombardy (chapter 1) was a typical case of overcoverage, because people who should have been counted as healed were actually considered still infected. On the contrary, an example of non-selection errors is selective recording (Cicourel, 1995). Selective recording refers to the use of non-registered information to define a situation and record the respective data. All secondary data may suffer from this problem, and it is useful to estimate its effect on our data. Selective recording was firstly distinguished by Cicourel (1995), who explained that when he was analysing data for his juvenile justice book, he found it difficult to disentangle why in some cases the police decided not to file a petition to juvenile court and give the juvenile "another chance". According to him, decisions were often arbitrary because no coding category was adequate to capture the variation that emerged. This is a common problem when using fixed-choice questions. The coding strategies are necessary to commensurate data, but often misrepresent the reality. Moreover, selective recording may be employed to hide some information. As Lauriault (2012) notes, indeed, users of data should not forget that databases are the results of shaping what question can be asked, how they are asked, how they are answered, how the answers are deployed, and who can ask them.

Timeliness

Algorithms and big data are said to allow a rapid and almost real-time analysis of phenomena with consequent decisions. Timeliness, however, is not always a dimension of data quality that is easy to fulfil also because it is highly related to all the other dimensions of data quality. Accurate data often need much time, and the need for comparable data may slow data collection. In addition, timely data require a high level of accessibility. Sagiroglu and Sinanc (2013) explain the differences in timeliness according to how data are stored. Batch systems update databases regularly, on a programmed time interval. It is the case for population registers and other private and administrative archives, where data are updated in large batches when the activities of the administration are suspended. Furthermore, there are real-time systems, which return already analysed data at the time data are registered plus the time that is needed to perform that analysis. Finally, data streams return data without a lapse between registering the data and giving back to the users. Kitchin (2014) noted that the management of vast amounts of continuous data is a technical challenge that public bodies are often ill-equipped to face, but the monitoring of phenomena in real time or near to real time has been widely acknowledged as the crucial change in policymaking created by big data methodologies (Hochtl et al., 2016; Aragona and De Rosa, 2017). Timely big data, which allows policymakers, civil servants, and citizens to take informed and organised collective decisions almost in real time, is a fundamental rhetoric that justifies the use of algorithmic decision systems. One example is smart cities, where the placement of always-on instruments such as sensors, video-surveillance cameras, and city services apps is increasingly promoted to intervene on security, pollution, traffic, etc.

Comparability

The comparability of data concerns the assessment of the effect that the differences in the operational definitions and applied concepts have on the possibility of comparing the data. Comparability does not exist in absolute terms, but only in "degrees of comparability". The problem of comparability arises from differences in criteria for constructing the data. In particular, difficulties may arise in comparing both data produced diachronically from the same source and data produced synchronously by different sources. The lack of comparability is due to the methodological aspects that frame the data (e.g., choice of indicators, operational definitions, units of analysis, time reference) and the effective collection strategies (selection choices, data collection instrument, data processing, etc.). Metadata may increase comparability and allow for better integration of data coming from different sources. Metadata are data about data and are provided for making clear use of the data without ambiguity and misinterpretation. Metadata turn out to be extremely helpful when data are organised into data infrastructures, such as data warehouses, informative systems, dashboards, and archives, where data coming from different datasets merge into a unique data setting. In all these cases, a careful process of documentation and standardisation of definitions and coding must take place to assure comparability between data.

The need for fully comparable data has been recently evoked to draw a contagion scenario at a global scale that will help supranational authorities (e.g., the WHO) to take coordinated actions to tackle the COVID-19 pandemic. For example, the metadata with all the European definitions that are applied to COVID-19 deaths have been collected by the WHO statistical office, and its comparison illustrated, among other things, differences in counting deaths. There are two main ways in which COVID-19 deaths are defined. The first, which adopts the WHO definition, uses clinically confirmed or probable COVID-19 case (e.g., Belgium, Canada, France, Germany) and is not dependent on the availability of a laboratory test. The second, on the other hand, is reliant primarily on a positive laboratory test (e.g., Austria, Italy, the Netherlands, Spain, the United Kingdom). Only through documentation and metadata it is possible to inspect the process of data construction so that differences in data may be understandable and explained, also because of the different degrees of comparability.

Relevance

If we can roughly say that accuracy, timeliness, and comparability refer to the production of the data, there are some other dimensions of data quality, relevance, and accessibility, that rather concern their possibilities of use. Relevance is generally defined as the correspondence of data with the objectives of data users. Trivellato (2002) clarifies that the data that respond to some objectives and needs may not be relevant for other specific objectives. For example, it is noted that in the EU many statistical data that are relevant to the European Commission are not relevant at all to local governments that need to collect their own data to analyse needs and to monitor and evaluate policy. By considering the relevance of data to various subjects, we recognise that anyone can approach data on equal terms; that is, data should be considered as public goods. The value of public goods is inverse to their scarcity; the more the good is diffused, the higher its value. Conversely, data are often seen as a private good, and especially in the big data domain, those few who own them have the interests to give value to this good on the basis of scarcity. Thus, the rarer the good, the higher its value. To assess the relevance of data, we should ask who exactly the users are and what objectives they really have. It is not possible that the same data are relevant for all users. For example, the data that are inputted in the COMPAS software in principle may serve different objectives than those of courts. Attorneys can analyse them to assess the profile of their defendants, or state prisons may draw information about the level of risks of their prisoners. However, this hardly happens, because those data are built to address specific questions and not others. Relevance must then be assessed by clarifying the main and the secondary purposes.

Accessibility

Accessibility refers to the physical means by which users can obtain the data (where to go, how to order, types of formats [microdata and macrodata available, etc.]). It is a fundamental issue, and in recent years, at least for data generated by public-funded research or by public agencies, some access criticalities have been overcome through open data initiatives and the building of data archives and data infrastructures that aim at sharing and making data available. The accessibility of government data by citizens, businesses, and other stakeholders, however, is contingent upon the provision of data in formats and procedures that allow the data to be used by anyone and for all potential purposes. Main features of accessible data comprise providing them free of charge, with unrestricted access, and in machine-readable formats. According to OECD (2015), many countries have started to employ their open data platforms to engage with citizens, researchers, and other stakeholders and give access to their data. However, access to the data of algorithms is sometimes perceived as critical because of privacy concerns. Privacy breaches may arise both when personal data are treated as part of the governmental process and when these are released to third parties for public scrutiny. One example of the former is what happened in the Netherlands when the Dutch government started to use the System Risk Indication (SyRI) to detect welfare fraud. The system had access to and processed data about work, fines, penalties, taxes, properties, housing, education, retirement, debts, benefits, allowances, subsidies, permits, and exemptions, and it was allowed to cross-refer data to spot "unlikely citizen profiles" that needed further investigation (Vervloesem, 2020). SyRI has been implemented without any transparency for citizens about what happened with their data, and on 5 February 2020, the Dutch court of The Hague ordered the immediate halt of SyRI because it violates Article 8 of the European Convention on Human Rights (ECHR), which protects the right to respect for private and family life.

A different privacy problem happens when training data are made accessible to third parties. Sensitive data are often required for detecting and seeking to ease algorithmic bias, posing practical and legal questions. In Europe, for example, the check for algorithmic bias using data about ethnicity or health would require explicit consent of the data subject under the GDPR. Various proposals have been made to address this kind of privacy issue, most of them anonymising the training datasets and the generated models (Shokri and Shmatikov, 2015).

The model

Auditing the algorithm's model consists of the definition of the attributes to associate with algorithm success, how they relate to this success, and the means used to optimise and calibrate the model. As said before, the final model is the result of a series of discussions, compromises, and negotiations between the different human (computer scientist, data scientist, domain experts, etc.) and non-human (platforms, codes, software, etc.) actors who participate in the co-construction of the algorithm. There are many reasons for auditing models.

First of all, despite their presumed impartiality, models reflect objectives and values, which should be made explicit. O'Neil (2016) considers algorithms as opinion formalised in code, and the definition of the success of a model is also a matter of opinion. The achievements of a model are often counted in terms of profit, but this form of success cannot be the standard for public algorithmic models. She, for example, explains that when people in the United States look for information about food stamps on a search engine, they are often confronted with ads about sites that look official and provide links to real government forms. But they offer people services that are not really needed and that can hardly be afforded. She asks if the fact that people click on these ads can be regarded as a success of the model. Maybe, from the point of view of Google, the answer is yes, but if we count success with a different lens, that of societal values, then the result is far from a success. Obviously, the algorithms employed in the public sector should pursue societal rather than market values. This makes the measurement of success much more difficult, because concepts like equity, fairness, and social good struggle with commensuration and quantification.

A further point is that it is difficult to evaluate the success of a model when it is based on machine learning. Machine learning is the process of solving a practical problem by gathering a dataset and algorithmically building a statistical model based on that dataset. These models may feed pernicious feedback loops. For example, going back to the recidivism algorithms, a man who scores as "high risk" is usually unemployed and from a poor neighbourhood, and he is likely to get a longer sentence and be imprisoned for years in a prison where he is surrounded by fellow criminals. When he will be released into the same poor neighbourhood, with a criminal record, it will be even harder to find a job. If he then commits another crime, the recidivism model can collect another success. But actually, it is the model itself that activate this chain reaction. Human scrutiny helps in detecting such model loops, but, unfortunately, the trend towards automation makes this more and more difficult, as computers have started to "learn" without human interventions not only from data in numerical forms but also from our written and natural language.

Finally, models should be audited because they can be wrongly designed and run. For example, the technical expertise requested by the Italian regional court and offered by the University of Tor Vergata in Rome (Salvucci et al., 2017) certified that two different programming languages were used in the algorithm that assigned teachers in Italian schools: the COBOL, now replaced by new programming languages, and C. Even in light of the simplicity of the requested operation, it is still not clear what are the reasons that led the programmers to create a pretentious and redundant programme that is not oriented to the maintainability model. This is also in consideration of the fact that it is statistically proven that a software that must perform elementary operations from the logical point of view, if it consists of a large number of lines of code, is more likely to lead to errors and malfunctions. Having articulated an algorithm that had to perform relatively simple functions in this way – the Roman engineers underline – is also a signal of a confused and fragmented work, handled several times over even by different programmers who have observed different standards of description. So, models can be written wrongs; therefore, they must be audited.

Another recent example is the Australian Online Compliance Intervention, known as "Robodebt" (Whelan, 2020). In July 2016 the Department of Human Services (DHS), to reduce expenses and eliminate undue payments, prepared a system that minimises the human control over any discrepancies. A large number of citizens are thus identified who will have to repay the sums received. The number of corrective interventions increased dramatically, from 20,000 per year to 20,000 per week, according to the enthusiastic commentary of the then Minister for Human Services, Alan Tudge (Senate Community Affairs Committee Secretariat, 2017. It was discovered, after many complaints, that the system had been poorly designed, because it used averaged income data to generate debt notices. This exposed the government to collective action: the proposed agreement between the petitioners' lawyers and the Commonwealth cost a total of about 770 million euros, including repayments for more than 460 million to 373,000 people, 71 million in compensation to approximately 400,000 people, and 254 million in cancelled debts (Gordon Legal, 2021). The analysis of the models can help in suggesting updates and adjustments – what is known as a dynamic model – but we must be clear in saying that there still will always be errors, because models cannot exactly fit the reality; they must simplify the complexity of the real world. Our duty as algorithm auditors would be advising about the consequences of the choices that are made to design the model and claim for clarity and openness so anyone can know it and understand it. Whether the success of a model is a matter of opinion, its transparency is a matter of ethics, equity, and right.

Fairness

Algorithms may systematically disadvantage different social groups and demographics. Friedman and Nissenbaum (1996) pointed out that computer systems can "systematically and unfairly discriminate against certain individuals or groups of individuals in favor of others" (p. 332). The need for fairness arises from the social values that worldwide have inspired many pieces of legislation about equality of rights, which define "protected characteristics" upon which it is illegal to discriminate against an individual (e.g., age, gender, disability, race, religion, etc.). Special attention is due to the issues of discrimination when public entities exercise their functions. In principle, the checking of algorithmic discriminatory decisions based on a protected characteristic could seem easy, but in practice, it is not, as many of these attributes may be strongly correlated within datasets (Rovatsos et al., 2020). If an algorithm is explicitly designed to neglect data on sex, and if this characteristic is strongly correlated with another attribute, such as part-time, it may still come to sex-biased decisions, but by proxy rather than directly.

Many technical approaches have been developed to detect bias in algorithms and related technologies. Kleinberg et al. (2016) propose three formal definitions that are commonly used: anti-classification, outcome/error parity, and calibration. Anti-classification means that the model is fair if it does not take into account protected characteristics or proxies from which protected characteristics can be inferred. Outcome/error parity means that a model is fair when protected groups receive equal rates of positive outcomes and/or errors. Algorithms are instead well-calibrated when, for example, the risk scores it gives to people reflect the actual outcomes in real life for the people given those scores. Equal calibration means that the percentage that results in the predicted outcome should be the same between groups (e.g., men and women).

The critical point with all these fairness measures is that they are often mutually exclusive. For example, as noted above when discussing the COMPAS algorithm, classification error parity is incompatible with calibration. *Propublica* noted that black defendants were almost twice as likely as whites to be labelled a higher risk of recidivism, but not actually reoffend. At the same time, Northpointe argued that the algorithm was not unequal because the reoffending rate was approximately the same regardless of the defendant's race; a high score predicted the same probability of reoffending. In pursuing calibration, the possibility of pairing errors may be reduced. Further, anti-classification may even be harmful to the groups intended to be protected. For example, as noticed before, women work part-time more often than men, meaning that if sex is excluded from a tool for assigning leave hours for family care, women will overall receive disproportionately fewer leaving hours than men. To really pursue fairness, these trade-offs must be weighed and balanced according to the specific context in which the system is used. Algorithms cannot be generically "fair" or be optimised towards all metrics of "fairness" simultaneously. Negotiations about what reasonably constitutes fairness are needed in all decision-making contexts.

All this means that fairness is overall a political concept rather than a technical one (Wong, 2020); the decision about the type of fairness essentially involves the choice between competing values. The task then is not merely improving the algorithms to satisfy some fairness measures, but to understand how to adapt diverse and conflicting interests. It is the very idea of fairness that should be questioned and settled before algorithms are put into practice. Thinking of only the technical challenges of algorithmic fairness discourages the critical reflection and the definition of fairness for public debate (Skirpan and Gorelick, 2017).

Understood as such, the actions to mitigate unfairness should concentrate on social and political rather than technical practices. The first of these is explicability. The EU GDPR and the Data Protection Act 2018 (which implements the provisions of the GDPR in the United Kingdom) at least theoretically mandate a "right to explanation" with regards to automated decision-making and the right to opt out of automated decisions. But how is it possible to explain that a model makes certain choices? It depends on the model. While it is somehow simple to describe deterministic models because they may be pictured through a decision tree, where you can track each decision's consequences on the following piece of the model, it is much more difficult to explain machine learning models, where releasing the model is unlikely to provide significant transparency.

A further action towards fairness concerns the increasing involvement of stakeholders and the ones impacted by algorithms through workshops and focus groups. Such encounters will facilitate in sharing views with the developers and find ways to embed the opinions of stakeholders into the development of the model. This also helps to mitigate problems, because they would emerge before the model is implemented and thus could be addressed in the ongoing design of an algorithm. Involvement allows early detection of potentially problematic consequences, such as those related to training data sets and the potential bias against protected characteristics. As reported in the study of the Panel for the Future of Science and Technology (Koene et al., 2019), such involvement has challenges. Firstly, there would likely be a tension between transparency and accessibility to the algorithms because the involvement of stakeholders may affect institutional privacy. Furthermore, there needs to be reflection on how to present algorithms to stakeholders of varying technical literacy to provoke meaningful discussion. An interesting solution to mitigate unfairness is the development of a private–public partnership to audit algorithms. The city of Amsterdam is developing an algorithm audit in conjunction with KPMG and Cathy O'Neil, the author of *Weapons of Math Destruction*. Drawing on the lengthy experience in almost any type of audit of the consulting company and on the expertise of the critical algorithm scholar, the administration seeks to investigate exactly what could go wrong. The audit has been made public, so many people are focusing on it. The news about this initiative has already generated attention. The project is not finished yet, but it is helping in developing criteria to govern and assess algorithmic decision systems. On the one hand, it sets up criteria for building and continuous monitoring and control of algorithmic solutions and their performance; on the other hand, it develops tools for understanding the level of organisational readiness to implement algorithmic decision systems and for overseeing the design, implementation, and operation of algorithms and assessing their challenges.

Algorithmic impact assessment

Impact is the fourth element of the algorithm audit. Auditing algorithm also means to consider the consequences of algorithmic decision systems and their integration in the social environment.

In the state of Indiana, between 2006 and 2008, one million requests for health, food stamp, or economic aid were denied due to a computer system that interpreted any errors in applicants' forms as a result of "failure to cooperate". This is one of the examples that Eubanks (2018) illustrates to explain that automated systems have been quickly adopted by the public welfare services of all the American states. The automation's impact on the lives of poorer and more socially excluded citizens – primarily African Americans – has been severe. The system used in Indiana to manage eligibility for public services broke up the individual cases into a series of tasks to be distributed to different social workers, as in an assembly line aimed at depersonalisation of the individual (Eubanks, 2018, p. 62). Similarly, in Pennsylvania, the assignment of a "risk of maltreatment" coefficient to minors involved a high level of surveillance of their families and concerned only those followed by social services. The cases reported by Eubanks (2018) are just a few of the many examples that could be made to show that the use of algorithms and related data-intensive technologies in public services unequally impacts the different categories of citizens.

Algorithms impact not only targeted categories but also the public administrations themselves. Yeung (2018) sees this growing dependence on data-based systems and algorithmic processing as a paradigm shift in public administration, from "new public management" to what he calls "new public analytics". The new technologies would transform the government itself into a platform. For example, in her study of Swedish public employment services and their algorithmic automation practices, Kaun (2020) noted that machine learning and implemented forms of automated decision-making transform the organisation itself, with the greater delegation of tasks and decisions to algorithmic systems. This leads, as in the cases reported by Eubanks (2018), to a loss of autonomy and discretion in the decision-making process of public officials. If less discretion may be seen as a positive element of automation, in reality, it is perceived as the latest form of bureaucratic formalism. What has always been considered one of the limits of bureaucracy is pursued and acclaimed as a strength of the new public analytics? This seems to witness a further transformation of public service, oriented to control rather than support. Algorithmic decision-making can even be organised in such a way that it interrupts human decision-making (Bailey et al., 2020). This may generate ethical problems related to how any algorithmic work is coordinated. Embedding algorithmic technologies into public services necessitates human work, and some of this human work is informal and ongoing. The informal, invisible nature of the work can create problems for authority. As noted by Eubanks (2018) in the case of caseworkers and by Bailey et al. (2020) in the case of nurses, if these caring figures take time away from caring work in order to undertake algorithmic work, then "what effect does this have on their ability to discharge the caring duties to which they are formally held to account?" (Bailey et al., 2020, p. 21). The new configuration of human–machine interaction resembles a human-in-the-loop pattern (Gronsund and Aanestad, 2020), where humans become part of the algorithmic logic.

Algorithmic impact assessment should focus not only on the consequences of algorithms, but also on the choice of using algorithms in the first place. Broussard (2018) attacks what she calls techno-chauvinism – "the belief that technology is always the solution" (p. 7) – a narrative that prevails in platform capitalism. What is implied in the adoption of algorithmic decision systems is the conviction that new technologies, no matter what, may improve the quality of governance and build a better world. These beliefs are rooted in assumptions that, in many cases, do not have empirical evidence and for which sometimes there is even counterevidence, but they are sustained by a narrative that reduces the complexity of the phenomenon and sustains the adoption of technology. Far from being the miraculous cure for all problems, Broussard (2018) explains that what we call artificial intelligence is a set of statistical techniques with still limited applications, which depend on human work, make mistakes, and often end up reiterating partisan worldviews.

Conclusions

Algorithms are built, in Weberian terms, for instrumental rationality, but they are supposed to carry means of emancipatory rationality. The possibilities offered by algorithmic systems in collecting and analysing data should help organisations in making the right choice, monitoring and enhancing achievements, and streamlining processes. However, there is a lack of evidence, so all the emancipatory potential is just assumed.

The role of social scientists is crucial in searching for evidence about this. It is difficult to empirically isolate the wider socio-technical assemblages of algorithmic decision-making, and only proactive empirical research on these issues can help to understand impact, anticipate risks, and unethical consequences, suggest early interventions to avoid or mitigate them, foster resilience, and assess that transparent best practices are developed, implemented, and appreciated. The contextualised evidence produced from this research can finally show if data-intensive technology really has the kind of emancipatory power that it is supposed to have. Much research should thus be devoted to empirically assess if these latest technologies are able to fulfil what they promise. The focus of algorithm audit, in my view, is on the feedback loop that exists among data, knowledge produced upon those data, and the policy intervention. Data are not only structured by social, economic, and political frames, but are also framing social, economic, and political terrains (Aragona et al., 2018). The interaction among these three aspects may build tautological *dispositifs* that are going to define and legitimate the same regimes of truth from where they start (O'Neil, 2016). This is particularly true for data infrastructures. The fact that they collect, link, match, and sort data that are then exploited by means of indexes, reports, and visualisation is another way to legitimate established definitions of situations. Concepts such as success, enhancement, augmentation, failure, and so on are in fact empirically represented through these macrodata, and the access to the microdata where they originate from is often not available to the public. But we as social researchers know that macrodata are heavily affected by choices, selections, and model biases, even more than microdata. There is therefore the need to reconstruct the data, the model, the fairness, and the impact of a certain algorithm in a specific context and in given scenarios. It is necessary to think through the entire context before auditing algorithms. As O'Neil noted when talking about the Amsterdam audit procedure:

> Evaluating within a context sounds like a lot of work .... it is a difficult, slow and frustrating conversation but one that we really must have .... we have to ensure that our values are incorporated into the algorithms. That is a very difficult challenge.
>
> (Renzenbrink, 2020, p. 40)

Note

1 *Propublica* is a newsroom in New York that aims to produce investigative journalism in the public interest and has won several Pulitzer prizes.

3 How

Introduction

The methods for auditing algorithms may come from both the technical sciences and the social sciences. In this chapter, I only show how social research methods may be effectively employed for auditing algorithms, rather than dig into all the possibilities offered by the more technical methods. There are two reasons behind this choice. Firstly, I am not a technical scholar, so it is wise to leave this to others. Secondly, I believe that the technical methods for improving transparency and explaining algorithms have the underlying logics in common with the social research methods. Technical and social methods for auditing algorithms should then be better understood as two sides of the same coin and be performed together, because it is by their mutual results that a full understanding of algorithms and their consequences may be achieved. In the following sections, I briefly sketch the logics of some technical methods, explaining how they can complement social research methods in auditing algorithms, but I do not give much further detail.

In recent years, much research in computer science has been devoted to finding ways to improve algorithm understandability as the possibility to provide information about the link between the input and the output of algorithms. On the one hand, greater attention is given to the availability of codes, design documentation, and, in the case of machine learning, learning datasets. On the other hand, methods for delivering information behind the algorithm itself have been developed. These may be roughly divided into two main categories: interpretable models and model-agnostic methods (Molnar, 2019). Interpretable models use a subset of algorithms that create models that are understandable to anyone with advanced statistical knowledge. Linear regression, logistic regression, and the decision tree

DOI: 10.4324/9781003080381-3

are commonly used interpretable models. Model-agnostic methods instead work by changing the input of the algorithm and measuring changes in the output. They can be applied, for example, to supervised machine learning models (Ribeiro et al., 2016) to assess how changes in the training data may alter the results. These two methods for improving the understandability of algorithms have underlying logics that are similar to those of the social research methods. Interpretable models recall the kinds of narratives that result from qualitative techniques, which centre the analysis of algorithms on their definition and meaning. On the contrary, model-agnostic methods aim to an explanation that can be either global (about the whole algorithm) or local (about specific results). However, they involve the same logic of, for example, quantitative methods, where changes in the independent variable (the input) explain changes in the dependent variable (the output). Of course, I do not want to say that social and technical methods for auditing algorithms do the same things or that they come to the same conclusions, but just that their logic is somehow similar.

Moving to social research methods, which I master better, many social research methods may be useful for auditing algorithms. It is possible to classify all of them on the basis of two elements: (1) the level of unobtrusiveness and (2) if they require access to the algorithm assemblage. Unobtrusive methods collect data on research units that are not aware of being studied. They do not require active participation (feedback) from those being researched; they are non-reactive. Unobtrusive methods were originally presented by Webb et al. (1966) as complementary and not alternative to intrusive methods of research, namely interviews and experiments. They believed that the combination of unobtrusive and intrusive methods would have reached the best research results. The most important advantage of using non-reactive methods is that the researcher does not disrupt the behaviours of the subjects he/she is studying. There is no reaction to questions posed or observations made. Beside the advantages, a negative of using non-reactive methods is that the results of their analysis are an exclusive processing of the researcher, without any feedback from the subject of research. The unobtrusive deconstruction of algorithms, for example, through documentation analysis or code testing, might provide insights into the workings of an algorithm, but it provides few clues as to the intent of the algorithm designers. The risk is that the researcher may interpret results by adopting a self-referential approach that is based on beliefs that adhere only to his/her normative, cognitive, and emotional premises (Amaturo and Aragona, 2012).

As said before, access to the algorithm assemblage is a big issue when choosing the research method for auditing algorithms. The algorithm assemblage is the complex socio-technical system composed of many apparatuses and elements that are thoroughly entwined. Assemblages are responsive, dynamic and lively, and constantly reconfigured (Andrejevic, 2013), and each assemblage forms part of a wider frame of many other interrelated and interacting data assemblages and systems (Aragona and De Rosa, 2018). Algorithm assemblage is composed of human and non-human actors whose relationships materialise within the different entwined apparatuses. Accessing the algorithm assemblage provides a means of uncovering the story behind the production of an algorithm and questioning its purpose and assumptions. Examples of research within the algorithm assemblage are interviews with designers and coders or the ethnography of a coding team (Aragona and Felaco, 2019). In interviews, respondents are questioned as to how they framed objectives and translated them into code with respect to languages and technologies, practices, influences, and constraints (Diakopoulos, 2016).

The choice between the different social research methods, however, depends above all upon the objectives. Ethnography may be the best choice, for example, when research aims to retrace the values that inspired the algorithm or for understanding the meanings that designers give to the success of the algorithm. Differently, experiments are fruitful when testing for fairness and at any time researchers are interested in how changes in data may impact results. Experiments may also be used for measuring the impact on the organisation and its workers. According to Kitchin (2017), given that algorithms act in the world, it is important not only to focus on the construction of algorithms and their production within the assemblage, but also to examine how they are deployed outside the assemblage in the different domains to perform a multitude of tasks. One possible method to undertake such research is ethnographies of how people engage with and are constrained by algorithmic systems (Lenglet, 2011).

In the following sections, a sample of social research methods for researching algorithms will be presented. This does not mean to be exhaustive; it is just an overview of the methods that may serve the purposes of algorithm auditing. Qualitative as well as quantitative methods are considered, and they should not be thought as an alternative. Actually, to effectively audit algorithms, they should instead be wisely mixed, trying to exploit what every method can give as added value, but, at the same time, testing their reliability, alongside other research techniques. Scholars accustomed to social research methods will find redundant the first paragraphs of the following three sections, where I generically introduce the various techniques of research. I apologise for this, but these are intended for scholars who do not have a social science background. Social scientists can skip these and go directly to the application of the methods for the audit of algorithms.

Experiments

Cause–effect questions are typical in scientific research. Some examples are as follows: What effect does drug A have on patient B? How does attrition influence the velocity of fast trains? How does a student's race affect his/her school results? How may a food programme impact on poverty? One of the possible ways to estimate casual effects is finding patterns in data. For example, you can calculate that minority students perform lower than others. However, this correlation is not sufficient for stating that race causes underperformance, because other variables may come into play in this link. It could be that an intervening variable bridges the relationship between these two phenomena, such as low-income neighbourhoods. Students coming from low-income neighbourhoods are more likely to underperform, and it may be that it is because minorities are more likely to live in low-income neighbourhoods that they systematically underperform in school. The solution to eliminate the problem of the intervening variables is to compare groups where differences are controlled for, such as by comparing low- and high-income neighbourhoods to see if the link between the two variables remains. However, it could be that other intervening variables alter the link between the two.

The only way of controlling for all intervening variables at the same time is therefore building equivalent groups that differ for just one characteristic (the treatment variable/the cause) and observing the differences in the experimental variable (the effect) between the group that received the treatment (experimental group) and the group that did not receive it (control group). This method is known as a randomised controlled experiment (Fisher, 1935). An experimental design has to fulfil several conditions. First of all, the units must be randomly selected from the population of the study. Furthermore, the selected units must be randomly assigned to the two groups. Thirdly, one of the two groups randomly gets the treatment. Finally, the outcome of this treatment must be measured. This research method can take the form of an artificial experiment, carried out in a laboratory scenario, or a natural experiment implemented in a real-life context. It can be run in analogue form or digital environments (Salganik, 2018).

The literature presents several taxonomies, from which three main types are considered (Lavrakas, 2008). The first is the true or classic experimental design that fulfils all four characteristics. Then, there are pre-experimental designs that do not have a control group. Thirdly are quasi-experimental designs, where units are not randomly extracted in the first place, but randomisation remains for assigning them to the two groups and giving treatment.

The applications of experiments for obtaining evidence about the functioning of algorithms may be various and applied to the datasets, to the targets of algorithms, or to the workers of the organisation impacted by the algorithm. A recent quasi-experiment that revealed bias in the algorithm was run by Ilinca Barsan (2021), director of data science at Wunderman Thompson, a marketing company that was developing a tool that would allow authorities to connect to thousands of street cameras and determine the proportion of pedestrians wearing masks at any given time. The computer vision Application Programming Interfaces (API) offered by Google, Microsoft, and IBM were intended to power the mask detection tool. However, they all exhibit gender bias when tested on self-portraits of people wearing partial face masks. Barsan firstly noticed this when uploading a photo of herself wearing a mask to test Cloud Vision API's accuracy. She was surprised by one of the labels, "duct tape", with an associated level of confidence of 96.6%. She continued testing the tool by wearing a ruby-coloured mask and a blue surgical mask. In these cases, the levels of confidence for "duct tape" were 87% and 66%, respectively, but quite surprisingly, the label mask, which in the first case was applied at 74%, was not applied at all. To test whether Cloud Vision API might classify appearances differently for mask-wearing men versus mask-wearing women, Barsan and her team constructed an experiment based on two groups of 265 images. The final corpora consisted of 265 images of men in masks and 265 images of women in masks in varying contexts, dressed differently, and with different kinds of masks. Out of the 265 images of men in masks, Cloud Vision API correctly identified 36% as containing personal protective equipment (PPE) and guessed that something covering a man's face was likely to be facial hair (27%). Around 15% of images were misclassified as "duct tape". But out of the 265 images of women in masks, Cloud Vision API returned PPE 19% of the time and mistook 28% as depicting duct tape. Facial hair was guessed as less probable (8%). For women, duct tape was a guess for labelling face masks at almost twice the number for men. This raises doubts about the learning datasets.

The results may be partly caused by the learning data that are used for developing the machine learning algorithm implemented in Google

Cloud Vision. However, Google is not the only one with apparent bias in its computer vision models. After testing Cloud Vision API, Barsan and her team ran the same dataset through IBM's Watson Visual Recognition service, which returned the label "restraint chains" for 23% of the images of masked women (compared with 10% of the images of men) and "gag" for 23% (compared with 10% of the images of men). The average confidence score for the "gag" label hovered around 79% for women compared to 75% for men, suggesting that Watson Visual Recognition was less biased than Cloud Vision API to assign those labels. In a conclusive experiment, Barsan and colleagues tested Microsoft's Azure Cognitive Services Computer Vision API. The tool correctly labelled only 9% of images of men and 5% of images of women. In this case, it did not return labels like "duct tape", "gag", or "restraint", but identified masks as "fashion accessories" for 40% of images of women (only 13% for men). Barsan explains that the results of these experiments are not a consequence of bad intents but are just evidence of the prejudices and stereotypes that can occur in unbalanced datasets and machine learning models. If she would not have run against this bias, and the tool for recognising how many people in a street wear masks would have been really developed, it cannot be excluded that it would have then been employed by local governments to control for the respect of safety rules. Experimenting with the tools on *ad hoc* datasets constructed for the purposes of the task may be the best research method to test for biases and the reliability of the system.

A completely different kind of experimental design may instead involve organisations rather than datasets and can be employed to estimate the impact that algorithms and other data-intensive solutions may have on the organisations that implement these solutions. For example, these designs are suitable to evaluate the opportunity of adopting algorithmic systems in the first place. Many failures of algorithmic systems occurred because the opportunity of using/not using these systems was not carefully tested. For example, in Italy, the adoption of the data infrastructure National Resident Population Registry (ANPR) was not having the results expected, but the government had no evidence of why that happened because no careful experimentation was designed. The ANPR is a centralisation project of the resident population registers that was launched in 2001. The regulation establishing the ANPR has entrusted the project to Sogei, the biggest state-owned Information Communication Technology (ICT) company. The initial project involved the creation of a single centralised web application (web app) for all of the more than 8,000 Italian municipalities. The first solution had the objective of producing greater cost savings, but it was not successful, as the municipalities already had software solutions that covered a range of ICT services and procedures greater than that envisaged by Sogei. The transition to the web app would therefore have led to a reduction in digitised services or the need to modify a large number of applications that interfaced with the register, such as marital status, taxes, and social services.

In 2017, Sogei stated that the project was concluded even though only one municipality of a few thousand inhabitants had migrated to the ANPR platform. The failure of the ANPR project was due to the insufficient attempt to meet the needs of the municipalities, carrying out a top-down strategy,. The problem was not technological, but social and organisational. In fact, the datafication of administrations requires not only good technology, but rethinking the overall organisation of the production, processing, and enhancement of data, with particular attention to the social context in which the infrastructure must be lowered, which is not only the technological ecosystem. It is instead a socio-technical system that is multi-actor (which sees the collaboration of PAs with private companies in the ICT sector), multilevel (which acts not only on the single PA, but also on all those connected to it; for example, the ANPR acts on the Ministry of the Interior, but also on all Italian municipalities), and multi-stakeholder (involving a series of stakeholders, both individual [citizens, users, employees] and collective [national and local governments, companies, NGOs]). If the Italian government in the first place had implemented the ANPR in a random sample of municipalities that varied in size, geographical area, level of digital services already offered to citizens, and other variables of interest, and not implemented the ANPR in another random sample with the same number of municipalities with equivalent characteristics as the first sample, it would have been much easier to understand why the ANPR was adopted with difficulties by so many municipalities. It would have isolated the causal effect.

Finally, similar experimental designs can be run, for example, as reported by Eubanks (2018) in the case of welfare, when administrations may implement automated tools for managing citizens' requests. Automated solutions may have a great impact on workers of an organisation because they change their working routines and their duties within the workplace according to the greater delegation of tasks and decisions in algorithmic systems. By selecting a sample of workers and randomly assigning them to two groups with similar characteristics like sex, age, education, seniority in employment, or working role, it is possible to estimate how automated systems impact different groups of workers. These experiments run with people may also allow to measure what experimenters call the counterfactual impact. If one group does not employ the automated method, it is possible to estimate what could have happened without intervention. For example, we may find that the number of citizens who get welfare support is declining because of the decrease in welfare expenditures, not because of the automated system.

In conclusion, many possible experimental designs may be set up to gain evidence about the fairness of algorithms and the impact of automated and data-intensive solutions on territories, organisations, and people. At any time that automated decision systems, or other data-intensive technologies, are developed and deployed in administrations, a causal analysis of their effects should be run. Experiments may serve this cause, and their use for auditing algorithms should be encouraged. As seen in this section, experiments may, on the one hand, be run within the algorithm assemblage, intruding on the subjects of research, as in the last examples. Or, on the other hand, experiments may also be run in a completely unobtrusive manner, as in the case of Barsan, testing the algorithms outside their assemblage and without anyone's involvement. For their flexibility of use, experiments represent a valuable method for researching algorithms and related technologies.

Ethnography

Ethnography is a research method that aims at describing the characteristics of culture, understood as a set of practices, knowledge, meanings, and values that describe individuals and the community/society they belong to (Dal Lago and Biasi, 2014). Ethnography explores cultural phenomena from the point of view of the subject of the study, and the data are collected often through participant observation, a technique that sees the researcher participating in the contexts with the people being studied, and documenting practices of interactions in their local contexts. But the physical presence of the researcher in a setting is not always demanded; there is ethnographic research that simply relies on interviews or documents. This research method has its origin in cultural anthropology in the early twentieth century, but it has been widely used in sociology for the analysis of subcultures and countercultures. Much ethnographic research is now run online (Caliandro, 2018). A specific type of ethnography, focused ethnography (Knoblauch, 2005; Gobo, 2008), consists of a time for observation, generally not participant, that is shorter than usual ethnography. Focused ethnography was first employed in organisational studies

(Hughes, 1970), and it is based on preliminary knowledge of the object of study.

Applying ethnography to the study of algorithms means to treat them as objects of cultural inquiry rather than as technological tools that are created and work in isolation. On the one hand, algorithms can be conceived as cultural objects because they involve beliefs, values, visions, and the background knowledge of their designers; on the other hand, algorithms can be regarded as cultural objects because they are also part of users' daily practices. Intending to uncover the story behind the production of an algorithm and to understand the human sensemaking that pervades its processes and operations, doing an ethnography of algorithms means spending time within a coding team, observing their work, and attending team meetings. At the same time, an ethnographic approach to algorithms should also include the everyday practices where algorithms are brought into use, entering the ordinary lives of the subjects of study. These two ways of entangling algorithms and culture may require different research strategies that we could call "ethnography of algorithms in the making" and "ethnography of algorithms in use" (Aragona et al., 2020). They are not properly two distinctive research strategies, but they may be seen as two end points of the same continuum, where various intermediate forms of ethnography may be placed. Ethnography of algorithms poses some peculiar challenges in both theoretical and methodological terms, which need to be discussed openly. According to whether we are interested in an ethnography of algorithms *in use* (by users) or an ethnography of algorithms *in the making* (by designers), these challenges may be faced differently. If the meaning of technologies depends on how individuals, groups, and institutions interact with them over time (Knorr-Cetina, 1999), then the designers, creators, and owners of algorithms can offer only a partial account of their role in society. Algorithms should be studied with the actors who use them. The everyday practices through which people engage with algorithms would then be considered as a constituent part of the algorithm itself (Introna, 2016).

Here are two examples of how ethnography may be employed for understanding the increasing use of algorithms in healthcare. The first study is about ethnography of algorithm in use, while the second one is about ethnography of algorithms in the making.

In both popular and academic discussions of the use of algorithms in clinical practice, narratives often draw on the decisive potentialities of algorithms and come with the belief that algorithms will substantially transform healthcare. Torenholt and Langstrup (2021) carried out an ethnography to explore how algorithms for clinical decision-making are enacted by healthcare professionals. They observed the development and implementation of patient-reported outcomes (PRO) tools in Denmark, tools that perform algorithmic sorting in clinical practice. They work within two disease areas – heart rehabilitation and breast cancer follow-up care – finding how the legitimacy of delegating to an algorithm is negotiated and obtained. What the study showed is that the values through which algorithmic systems are promoted and sustained change between the different communities of stakeholders involved. While, at the health governance level, algorithms constitute tools for dismissing inefficient work, at the level of physicians, these tools represent everything but the disruption of their activities. Instead, they are legitimated as a continuation of standardised and systematic clinical activities for producing evidence-based diagnostic procedures that reinforce the physicians' expertise and authority. The authors conclude that between the two different communities of stakeholders, two divergent legitimation narratives are in place, but both provide a push towards the use of algorithms in healthcare.

Murero (2020) conducted an auto-ethnography (Anderson, 2016) of a health algorithm in the making. The algorithm to be adopted in Berlin hospitals was intended to forecast cardiovascular disease on the basis of a set of parameters extracted through machine learning from the records of patients who got ill in the past. Also, in this case, ethnography was adapted because the author wanted to observe algorithm design as the result of negotiations between multiple cultures, a heterogeneous ecosystem that competes and collaborates in complex infrastructure of practices, human and non-human (Seaver, 2013). For example, Murero shows how the different expert communities reacted differently about the important issue of privacy that the management of a huge amount of sensitive health data had caused. While security experts pointed out the problem of asking for consent, the computer scientists were concerned with the possibilities of merging a large quantity of datasets built on different and sometimes conflicting digital systems. Physicians wanted instead to overcome all the troubles with the data in order to run the models and see if the algorithm could really save lives. Access to public health data for training algorithms emerged as the result of a cooperative agreement of forces that requires systems of power negotiation and authorisation. The author finally argues that the design of algorithms in healthcare is the final output of what she calls complex socio-tech-med cultures. She shows how the logics embodied in the algorithms are not only driven by mathematical formulas, machine language codes, and electronic impulses, but are also regulated by human actions mediated by the cultural practices of specific expert communities.

Ethnography is an intrusive method that requires access to the settings where individuals act. If the objective of ethnography is understanding how people engage or resist algorithms, the study may require observation in multiple settings, in different situations and locations. On the contrary, ethnography of algorithms in the making requires access to the overall assemblage, which can be difficult to obtain. Access may depend on influence, budget, and goals; may be individually negotiated; and requires signing a series of agreements concerning intellectual property and non-disclosure. This is particularly the case when it comes to proprietary algorithms (Van Couvering, 2007). In this case, interviews and observation take place in fully organised settings and are planned far in advance. Researchers must be very skilled in finding the right gatekeepers who can negotiate the conditions of their participation. Sometimes gatekeepers may be concerned about the damage to the image of the owners of the algorithm and the internal contrasts that may arise as a result of the inclusion of the researcher. Success is dependent on the ethnographer's ability to persuade the gatekeepers that there might be mutual gains for the owners, reaching the point of establishing an agreement. Finally, studying algorithms in the making creates problems of language that are quite different from the usual problems faced by those who study algorithms in daily use. It is not just a matter of the intricate language of coding: the multi-layered structural complexity of the assemblage, which sees the participation of several expert teams that make technical decisions according to different knowledges, languages, and skills, makes the socio-technical core of algorithms mostly inaccessible to non-experts. In this case, mediation is crucial. Mediators can help in understanding how different communities of experts interact in the assemblage, translating their technical languages into ordinary language.

Survey

Survey is probably the most used social research method. Survey, through the adoption of standardised data collection procedures and the extraction of a representative sample of selected individuals from a larger population, allows statistical elaboration of a series of properties previously identified by the researcher, with the aim of investigating relationships between variables. The standardisation of the data collection procedure is guaranteed by the use of a questionnaire that is carefully defined about what to gather (the concepts); the means in which the questions will be asked (wording and order);

the rules for managing the questionnaire and the rules for managing the interaction, if any, between interviewer and interviewee; and the ways in which the answers to the questions must be provided (closed vs open answers). Since data are collected using standardised tools, procedures, and rules, it is possible to compare data about different cases (subjects). It is precisely based on the possibility of comparing the answers of the various interviewees that statistical techniques of analysis may be employed. The goal of standardisation is that each respondent be exposed to the same question, so that "any difference in the answers can be correctly interpreted as reflecting differences between respondents rather than differences in the process that produced the answer" (Fowler and Mangione, 1990, p. 14).

Digital technologies enable new opportunities for survey research. First, the digital offers new avenues for administering questionnaires as, for example, web surveys. These entail obvious advantages, such as reduction of the time required for the survey, reduction of costs, fast statistical processing, and the possibility of customising the survey questionnaire. Today, there are numerous online platforms that support the construction and dissemination of web surveys by means of emails, links, and social media. Furthermore, interesting ways of asking are emerging, such as Wikisurvey (Salganik and Levy, 2015). Open questions and closed questions can give very different information. Open questions are rarely used because they are difficult to analyse, but they can be the most interesting ones because they open to the context of discovery (Reichenbach,1938). Wikisurveys allow the researcher to enrich the possible answers to questions over time based on the answers of the participants to open questions. In New York, they were used to incorporate citizens' ideas into the city's sustainability plan. When asked about better ways for creating a bigger and greener New York, 25 ideas were presented, but as citizens asked for their ideas to be included, after the approval of the administration they appeared among the possible answers. Following the logic of Wikipedia, in practice, everyone can add a piece of the possible answer to a question. Gamification is another interesting example. In this case, the basic idea is that if you use games for asking questions, people are more keen to answer about serious themes.

The application of survey to algorithms and related technologies is justified every time there is the objective of collecting opinions, attitudes, and behaviours of individuals impacted by automation. In 2012 the Piedmont Regional Government ran a survey consultation campaign to collect attitudes about the adoption of a telemedicine platform that allows regional physicians to perform preliminary online anamneses (Ferro et al., 2013). Telemedicine had already been experimented in 2008 in one of the least populated and most mountainous of its provinces: Verbano–Cusio–Ossola (VCO). This pilot went well, and it was decided to establish a consultation campaign using a web survey posted on multiple social media, aiming at exploring the possibility to implement the telemedicine initiative in the whole region. The survey had the objective to measure the level of acceptance of this telemedicine policy as well as the will to pay for its implementation (e.g., cover personal costs of device rental, internet connection, etc.). The results from the analysis of citizens' responses to the web questionnaire highlighted that the idea was received very positively by 94% of the respondents. In addition, 62% declared willingness to co-finance the implementation of the solution. The analysis of citizens' opinions gave useful insights on the outputs expected from this telemedicine policy and, at the same time, on possible difficulties and required developments. The citizens who took part in the campaign outlined "the risk of applying a technocratic approach that does not take into account the human aspects of the physician–patient relationship" (Ferro et al., 2013, p. 365). According to the authors of the consultation, running surveys about such themes allows public sector ICT to be examined not only from an economic and efficiency perspective, but also from a public value perspective, with respect to its role in the production of social value. Some positive outcomes were identified by interviewees (rationalisation of public spending, reduction of queues in clinical examinations, patients' better quality of life, fewer trips to hospitals, and reduced CO_2 emissions). At the same time, negative impacts were envisaged by citizens, such as healthcare with fewer human relationships between patients and doctors or with less "physical examination". Positive and negative opinions can be useful for designing and readdressing public automating policies and for producing follow-up and evaluation that measure not only efficiency and spending but the social values that automation endorses.

The walkthrough method

A relatively new method that can be employed to acquire evidence about the functioning of automated systems and other algorithmic solutions is the walkthrough method. This method has been principally used for engaging directly with an app's interface to understand its technological mechanisms and embedded cultural references to discover how it guides users and shapes their experiences (Light et al., 2018). It consists of a step-by-step observation of the app's interfaces and screens. Initial uses of the walkthrough were grounded in software engineering and oriented towards improving the quality of code and user experience (Fagan, 1976), but this method has since been shaped by scholars at the crossroads between science and technology studies (STS) and cultural studies, so this is now adaptable to a range of research questions. The main objective of walkthrough is making explicit the ideology behind an automated solution and how this produces affordances within it. It critically examines the workings of systems as a socio-technical artefact. Walkthrough usually sees the researcher examining the system alone, but it can be run alongside users or even by the sole users. Researchers ask users to collect data about how registration, consent, privacy, and data transmission are arranged within the system, what options can be chosen, and what consequences these options have, for example, on the services the user can get. Walkthrough concentrates on the interface arrangement, the functions, and the text embedded in the interfaces (e.g., the drop-down menus). Users can be recruited both offline and online, for example, using crowdsourcing platforms such as Amazon Mechanical Turk. It is also possible to use personas, "the creation and use of fictional users, concrete representations" (Grudin and Pruitt, 2002, p. 1). Personas act in the system as archetypical users and allow researchers to see main characters, goals, and activity scenarios.

An interesting study that made use of a persona-based walkthrough method was conducted by Smith (2018) on the Geluksmeter, a system introduced by the Dutch Ministry of Internal Affairs in 2016, to visualise statistical data related to the happiness and well-being of Dutch citizens. Citizens can calculate a personalised happiness score by drawing on an underlying algorithmic system and dataset, which then is visualised in an interface. The data used for computing the score come from answers to eight simple questions based on certain dimensions. After answering these questions, the personal score is visualised within an infographic and can be compared with average scores relating to a specific gender, age, or territorial group. Measuring citizens' well-being is a global trend that has been pushed by the Sustainable Development Goals (2018) of the United Nations, but the difficulty of measuring such a multidimensional concept has been noted (Stewart, 2014).

Smith (2018) constructed four fictitious personas to understand how the Geluksmeter reconceptualises the notion of happiness, and depicted what makes the objectivity of happiness and what assumptions are embedded in the happiness meter, as well as how these assumptions imply and obscure the values and norms that influence the assessment of different citizen-archetypes. Results were very interesting. The system made many assumptions about users. A user should, for example, be a resident who does not reside in one of the public bodies, has a binary gender, and is age 18 or above. People 65 or above were assumed to be retired by the system, even if individuals of that age could be still working and active, which impacts happiness. The personas walkthrough method turned out to be significant in finding assumptions about automated systems that can limit action on the system to people with specific characteristics. The advantage of the walkthrough is that the researcher does not need to access the algorithm assemblage, and he/she does not contact the designers of the algorithm. A criticism concerns the choice of personas, which must be carefully designed.

Conclusions

The overview of social research methods for finding evidence about algorithms in this chapter must not be considered exhaustive. There are other strategies to conduct research designs that have the algorithm as the object of study. Social research methods may be useful for such a scope, and much research is needed in this emerging field to refine methods for auditing algorithms. This may give insights on how to design our technologies and how to develop policies to accompany them, instead of leaving these decisions to IT corporations. More critical research is needed, for example, on algorithmic fairness, explainability, and security. Researching algorithms and developing empirical insights about their production processes and use in society are possible strategies to raise awareness about algocracy, along with its intended and unintended consequences. Research on how algorithmic systems are built and used will contribute to giving us answers to relevant questions about privacy, freedom, and equality. In all this, the role of social researchers with expertise in methods (both quantitative and qualitative) is crucial to isolate the socio-technical assemblages in which automated decisions are made. The empirical analysis of algorithms starts with their critique, but it should aim not only to criticise them but also to make ourselves aware, reveal how they work, and understand the intended and unintended impacts on society. Only empirical research can allow us to put aside prejudice and instead enter into the merits of the functioning of these systems. Paradoxically, this could lead to more use of algorithms, perhaps better, more conscious, and critical use.

4   Rights, politics, and education

Introduction

Algorithm audit (AA) may have wide impacts on all the spheres of society. It is not possible to pursue transparency, accountability, and fairness of artificial intelligence (AI) and automation if we do not take into account the broader consequences that the development of methods for auditing algorithms has for rights, politics, and education. AA should not be deployed in isolation. It needs institutions, citizens, academics, and corporations; all stakeholders have to participate in it. Algorithms are not employed in a vacuum, and neither can AA be thought of as a stand-alone accountability practice. For AA to be a successful enterprise, we need to find means to co-create rules, processes, and methods.

A market will not regulate algorithms on its own. As O'Neil notes, "entire business and governance models .... are built upon them .... those raking in the profits think it's working just fine" (2016, p. 176). Governments cannot be passive. Many of the examples that I mentioned in the previous chapters (e.g., the Italian Buonascuola, the British Ofqual, the Australian Robodebt, the American COMPAS, the Dutch SyRI, etc.) show that often it is only when an undesirable outcome has occurred that public institutions take action. It would be much more sensible to respond to the risks of automation through prevention instead. Politics should recognise that the risks are a consequence of the increasing dependence of governance on algorithms and that this dependence can sometimes be avoided. Increasing dependence is nothing but an obligation; it is a deliberate choice made in the belief that new technical experts can solve old governance problems, such as efficiency and efficacy. What is needed most is probably competent government officials with the necessary education and training to drive the fourth revolution (Floridi, 2014) in

DOI: 10.4324/9781003080381-4

a reflexive and inclusive way: reflexive because governments should focus on determining what kind of algorithms can usefully be managed, at what policy level they are really demanded, how they can be integrated into the work of public administrations, by whom and for what purposes, and inclusive because true innovation starts with co-creation, in which all stakeholders are equal. The corporatisation of the public arena is something that we should fight not because corporations are evil but because, in social matters, stakeholders have to stay on the same level, and technology cannot drive governance and social change. Furthermore, inclusiveness means that we need to find the means to involve the affected targets. Participation in social life is crucial for gaining respect from others, and the basic opportunity to participate actively in algorithms' assemblage should be the right of everyone affected. However, effective participation means equipping individuals to understand the underlying principles and challenges of algorithms. It is only this understanding that will empower people to comprehend, interpret, and assess the algorithms that have targeted them. People's awareness of being a target and ability to protect themselves from algorithmic authority should be accompanied by proactive behaviour. However, as people do not know that they are affected, action "from below" will rarely happen.

Evidence is the key to explaining how algorithms exert an impact on policy results, how they can be employed in transparent processes of decision-making, and what citizens' perspectives on algorithmic governance are. The Science and Technology Options Assessment (STOA) unit of the European Parliament, in its study on a governance framework for algorithmic accountability and transparency (Koene et al., 2019), advocates the creation of a plan for providing access to outside researchers and auditors to "examine specific systems and gain a fuller account of their workings, and to engage the public and affected communities in the process" (p. 59). This access should be gained in a short time; the report suggests within six months of deployment. However, the study underlines that, while it can sometimes be possible for individuals and collective citizens' groups to examine the algorithms themselves, this cannot be the rule because they will not always have the time, the knowledge, and the resources necessary to assess algorithms. It therefore suggests granting access to qualified researchers, trusted external experts who can certify that algorithms are not harmful to citizens. The STOA study is one of the best documents supporting the auditing of algorithms, and its position is absolutely embraceable, but the fact that more experts are needed just shifts the focus of the problem. Who will decide who the experts are, what characteristics they should have, and how they should be trained? In this phase, in which automated systems are becoming widespread but definite training and specific political recognition of these figures are still lacking, the call for experts sounds like an intention rather than a concrete move towards the building of an efficient and independent auditing system. In fact, one can notice that some of the most careful analyses of algorithmic governance cases come from the worlds of journalism (Angwin et al., 2016; Kayser-Bril, 2020) and civic activism (Verdacht, 2021). We should therefore take more systematic action to tackle the risks of algorithmic governance that not only imagines a kind of super experts, but also activates a series of changes in the way in which algorithmic governance is understood at the legal, political, and educational levels.

What is taking place now worldwide with the spread of algorithmic technologies throughout public governance resembles what happened in 2008 with the financial crisis. When visiting the London School of Economics, Queen Elizabeth famously asked: "Why did nobody see it coming?"

Experts from the British Academy answered the Queen one year later by saying:

> Everyone seemed to be doing their own job properly on its own merit. And according to standard measures of success, they were often doing it well. The failure was to see how collectively this added up to a series of interconnected imbalances over which no single authority had jurisdiction. …. Individual risks may rightly have been viewed as small, but the risk to the system as a whole was vast. …. So in summary, Your Majesty, the failure to foresee the timing, extent and severity of the crisis and to head it off, while it had many causes, was principally a failure of the collective imagination of many bright people, both in this country and internationally, to understand the risks to the system as a whole.
>
> (Besley and Hennessy, 2009, pp. 2–3)

Returning to algorithms, we need to find ways to understand the risks of algorithms "as a whole". Risks of injustice have always existed, even when decisions were taken only by humans. The difference is that algorithmic risks are systemic. As O'Neil (2016) noticed, human decision-making evolves, while it is difficult to change automated systems, even if they are based on learning algorithms. Anyone who has ever participated in the assemblage of data and algorithms knows that any change costs time and money. As a result, despite their ambition to drive the future, algorithms are past oriented. They are based on data that often register past situations and employ the technological solutions available at the time. As a result, they can be repeatedly and uncritically used until a disruptive event takes place. It would be better not to wait for a troublesome crisis such as that of 2008 but to develop thoughtful and coordinated work now involving governments, corporations, academia, and citizens around three main intertwined pillars: rights, politics, and education.

Rights

How can innovation and its incredible potential be reconciled with the rigorous protection of individual guarantees and social rights? This is a difficult question to answer but an impossible one to avoid. The legislation on AI and automation is quite scattered worldwide, but there are some overarching principles that are included in almost every piece of regulation, from the Canadian *Directive on Automated Decision-Making* to the EU's *Ethics Guidelines for Trustworthy AI* and Singapore's *Model Artificial Intelligence Governance Framework*, just to mention a few. These include transparency and accountability, freedom and control of humans, and data protection and risk management.

A fundamental aspect of transparency and accountability is the fact that individuals' rights may be affected by governments. When algorithmic systems play a significant role in governments' decisions, the public should be given notice. Every public authority should publicly disclose its proposed and existing automated decision systems (ADSs), including their purpose, reach, type of data used, and potential impacts on communities or individuals. Tene and Polonetsky (2012) propose a new right to reasonable inference, which is appropriate for all the inferences performed resulting in inscrutable predictions that damage people's privacy and life. This right would require the entity employing automation to establish ex ante justification: why specific data are a relevant basis on which to draw inferences and why these inferences are relevant to the type of automated decision. The people affected should have the right to challenge unreasonable inferences. In the EU, this kind of right is linked to Art. 22(3) of the EU GDPR, which rules that

> the data controller shall implement suitable measures to safeguard the data subject's rights and freedoms and legitimate interests, at least the right to obtain human intervention on the part of the controller, to express his or her point of view and to contest the decision.

The introduction of the "right to reasonable inferences" could rule the use of machine learning methods that are currently not amenable to explanation, requiring an explanation for why data sources are selected and inferences are drawn prior to deployment at scale. As noted (Koene et al., 2019), however, such a right to reasonable inferences must be counterbalanced with the laws on intellectual property and trade secrets.

Algorithms can be protected in three main ways: through intellectual property, trade secrets, and patents. Confidentiality is the main method for preventing corporate competitiveness. The protection of patents has been used by the industry as an argument against algorithmic transparency, but, because patents are public, they do not constitute an obstacle to AA per se. Intellectual property and trade secrets may instead set limits on transparency and accountability. The details of algorithmic functioning are the core of ICT corporations, and their disclosure to society could damage businesses since this would make it possible for competitors to use the algorithm to their own benefit. There are still insufficient rights to ask companies for full disclosure of their algorithms without affecting their competitive strategies. There should be an overall rethinking of the legislation on intellectual property and trade secrets globally to safeguard algorithmic disclosure within confidentiality agreements.

For example, one of the biggest issues with the Ofqual algorithm presented in the introduction to the book was that the Royal Statistics Society, which wanted to give advice on the calculation of grades, decided not to be involved because of a non-disclosure agreement (NDA) that prevented it from commenting in any way on the final choice of the model for some years after the results had been released. The president of Ofqual, on the contrary, said that the NDA was a normal and entirely ethical mechanism to protect only confidential information. This would not have happened with a tighter regulation on how confidentiality should be handled when algorithms are used by public authorities and there is a need to be accountable to citizens and other stakeholders.

The final aspect that requires action is the labour law. According to an analysis by Deloitte and Oxford University, many public-sector jobs will be automated by 2030 (Smith, 2016). Administrative and operative roles, which account for 27% of the public workforce, are identified as having the highest probability of being automated. However, as we have already noticed in Chapter 2, algorithms may also affect workers with cognitive and social skills, such as social workers and police officers, as well as those with high-skill profiles, such as judges.

The challenge in these cases concerns both the tasks of workers and the accountability of their work. Regarding the tasks, jobs based on social utility and human interaction will probably be demoted to data entry and reporting. For example, in welfare work, the indiscriminate adoption of new technologies is resulting in "the progressive dematerialization and dehumanization of the relationship between the beneficiary of the service and the welfare worker" (Deriu, 2020, p. 256), whereby the social services cannot understand why a family has been identified for preventive intervention or why a contribution has been denied or revoked. Concerning accountability, as many sentences around the world have confirmed, public administrations are responsible for the decisions and impacts of their algorithms. Public workers will become accountable for activities and choices that are in fact guided by technology that they hardly understand because they have been trained in completely different skills. When human decision-making is highly integrated with algorithms, making it difficult to quantify the impact of the machine on the decisions with respect to humans, how can humans really be accountable for decisions taken on the basis of technologies to which they are not accustomed and trained to understand fully? This intricate human–machine accountability should be a lever for regulating the sector. If I am responsible for what is decided through automation, then I would ask my automated service provider to adhere to my rules of accountability and transparency. Otherwise, I cannot be fully responsible for my choice, can I? This is a very slippery piece of regulation to write, but it is something that regulators should think through carefully.

Politics

The development, deployment, and increasing use of algorithms and automated systems concern not only technology but also the socio-technical systems of which they are part, that is, the people, organisations, and societal contexts in which algorithms are implemented. The major challenge is not technological but political; it is about ensuring that algorithmic systems are aligned with human values and ethical principles. According to Forbes (Hirshon, 2019), of America's 50 most promising AI companies, only one, Aira, applies its algorithms for social good. Aira is a company that combines human beings and its AI-powered agent, Chloe, through its app or custom smart glasses to help people with blindness or low vision to sense the world better. The other 49 companies developed AI algorithms for driving cars, calculating risks, managing logistics, or saving money:

in one word, profit. There is nothing wrong with profit, but surely we cannot expect companies to regulate the market on their own. Politics has to step in to resolve the ethical issues that surround the use of algorithms and make the difference.

The document produced by the High-Level Expert Group on AI of the EU, *Ethics Guidelines for Trustworthy Artificial Intelligence* (Bergmann et al., 2019) – first drafted in December 2018 and receiving more than 500 comments through an open consultation – is the first important acknowledgement of the need to deal politically with all the challenges that ADSs and AI pose. The document focuses on two main important principles: first, AI and ADSs should put people first (technology should work for people); second, technology is not good or bad per se, but it is what you do with technology that becomes good or bad. As Von der Leyen puts it: "We want to encourage our businesses, our researchers, the innovators, the entrepreneurs, to develop Artificial Intelligence. And we want to encourage our citizens to feel confident to use it" (European Union, 2020, p. 2). What is innovative in the EU document is that it tries to implement the main principles of accountability, transparency, privacy, and fairness in practice by developing a checklist that guides developers and deployers of AI to self-assess the risks. For example, when talking about face recognition, a truly controversial issue, the document proposes a distinction between biometric "authentication", which is seen as non-controversial (e.g., face recognition to unlock a smartphone), and remote biometric "identification" (such as deployment in public squares to identify protesters), which could arouse serious human rights and privacy concerns. Only cases in the latter category would be problematic under the scheme proposed by the EU.

However, as the independent *Algorithm Watch* noted in its latest report, *Automating Society* (Chiusi et al., 2020), in all the EU documents on AI and ADSs, the risks associated with these technologies are generally considered as potential, while the benefits are represented as very tangible and direct. This has led some human rights activists to claim that the narrative of the EU suggests putting global competitiveness ahead of the protection of fundamental rights. Still, it must be recognised that some very foundational issues are raised in the documents. One is the focus on the interoperability of AI and ADSs and the creation of a network of research centres directed to applications aimed at excellence and competence building. Another highlights the difficulty of pursuing fairness for all. As the analysis of COMPAS revealed (Chapter 2), what is good for one person may be bad for another. Finally, it is necessary not to consider algorithmic unfairness separately from human unfairness. As shown throughout this book, many algorithmic systems have been introduced to overcome the limitations of human decision-making. For instance, the COMPAS algorithm was seen as a means to address the potential for bias in the reasoning of judges; similarly, the Ofqual algorithm was considered as a way to detach grades from individual teachers' evaluation. The promoters of these systems sponsor them because they save time, reduce human bias, and are free from discrimination. However, determining whether algorithms improve human decision-making or are superior to it has proven to be extremely difficult.

One way to increase the possibility of measuring the performances of algorithms on a "human values" scale is the establishment of a public register of the ADSs and AI employed in the public sector. As advocated by Algorithm Watch, the record should come with the legal obligation for those responsible for an ADS to disclose and document the purpose of the system and provide an explanation of the model (the logic involved) and information about who developed the system. The register should be easily accessible and give information on data and procedures. Another step towards AA is the foundation of a network of national and international authorities on algorithmic risk assessment. Building and developing regulatory bodies that can negotiate procedures, tools, processes, and all the necessary conventions to fix standards that ensure the quality of algorithms constitute a very reasonable aim. During the last decades of the last millennium, this institutional set-up served well in the case of statistical data. At that time, along with the restructuring of national statistics institutes, the networks of agencies devoted to the construction of data widened with the entrance of various international organisations, such as the United Nations, the European Union, the Organization for Economic Cooperation and Development (OECD) and the International Labour Organisation (ILO). That network was able to fix quality standards, for example, through the standard definition of the total survey error, to adopt shared classifications for units and variables (i.e., NUTS, NACE, ISCO, ISCED, etc.) and to define a common procedure for producing and exchanging metadata. The same should be undertaken for algorithms. A network of national algorithm authorities, linked to a few international authorities, would be a solution for populating the register of AI and ADSs, creating benchmarks and defining best practices. This, of course, should work not in isolation but in accordance with the already-existing data protection authorities (DPAs) and international standards organisations (ISOs), which can help in the standardisation of procedures and the definition of quality indicators.

This standard can be used for monitoring corporations and asking for mandatory impact assessments, as happens, for example, with environmental impact assessment.

The final political stance is to sustain people-centred co-creation (Voorberg et al., 2015) through greater citizen involvement. Co-creation refers to the active involvement of end users in various stages of the production process. More specifically, the type of co-creation that could be implemented is quadruple-helix co-creation (Arnkil et al., 2010), which aims to align the efforts of four main stakeholders (industry, government, academy, and citizens) to define a compelling shared vision. This model can work well with the intermediation of collective actors such as city councils and activists. Through co-creation, people are harnessed via commitment rather than compliance, resulting in strong synergies. The process of co-creation should be fuelled by evidence produced on the functioning of algorithms in different institutional settings and by research on needs assessment, community studies with ethnography, and quadruple-helix focus group interviews. Most importantly, however, to increase substantially the participation of end users in the algorithm assemblage, educational programmes aimed at expanding citizens' knowledge and skills in relation to algorithms, their functioning, and their possible risks should be actively sustained.

Education

The increasing transparency and accountability of algorithmic systems can really be useful only if governments are able to deal effectively with those systems and their impacts. In addition, the people affected by these systems need to understand the risks and opportunities of their deployment. This is why we need to enhance algorithmic literacy at all levels, for relevant stakeholders as well as citizens. Algorithmic literacy is not only about enabling individuals to master a particular skill or to become proficient in a certain technology but also involves equipping individuals to understand the underlying principles and challenges of algorithms. This understanding will in turn empower people to comprehend, interpret, and use the algorithms that they encounter, which is a prerequisite for algorithmic awareness (Britt-Gran et al., 2020). An awareness of algorithms means, on one side, having knowledge of being subjected to algorithmic systems but a limited ability to use algorithms (passive awareness) and, on the other side, that the knowledge of being affected is accompanied by proactive behaviour, for example, to protect data or to exploit the algorithm for personal or collective ends. Along with algorithmic awareness, algorithmic readiness on the side of institutions should be promoted. Algorithmic readiness indicates the degree of capability to take advantage of computation and to take informed decisions based on algorithmic systems. Algorithmic readiness consists of two main aspects: algorithmic culture and algorithmic governance. If the algorithmic culture is the level of development of algorithms in administrative processes and practices – which is affected by the algorithmic literacy of the people working for administrations – algorithmic governance refers instead to the overall management of quality and security of the algorithms employed by the administration – which is influenced by ecosystem constraints and by connections within the networks of actors (social and technical) that are involved in the algorithmic assemblage. In a context of algorithm-intensive societies, awareness and readiness are important means of promoting accountability and fairness, a doorway to understanding, interpreting, and managing automated decisions for all public administrations and citizens. As the STOA study (Koene et al., 2019) reports, enhancing the level of understanding of algorithmic systems is necessary but not sufficient, since many issues raised by such systems should be subject to public debate. To ensure the quality of this debate, it must involve a great variety of stakeholders' opinions and interests, including those of experts in several disciplines (technical as well as social), policymakers, professionals, Non-Governmental Organisations (NGO), and the general public. The risk of not involving all the stakeholders is that key issues may be overlooked, including the most important question of deciding whether to employ algorithms in the first place.

   Educating public workers and citizens would not be the only training challenge. In the context of algorithmic decision systems, algorithm auditing represents an area that implies new competencies. It is important to identify, underline, and accredit those new skills to stakeholders, both public and private. Algorithm auditing lies in the intersection between computer science, data science, social research methods, and automating ethics. It may be at the global (about the whole algorithm) or local (about specific results) level, and the strengths and weaknesses of each evaluation should be assessed regarding the stakeholders, their level of expertise, and their objectives (to challenge a decision, take actions to obtain a decision, verify compliance with legal obligations, etc.). AI and ADSs are complex, and checking that these systems serve the public sector fairly and ethically requires multiple skills. Critical thinking and logic come into play when determining the kind of scenarios to be tested and evaluating the outcomes against societal norms and values. Knowledge of regulations and ethics is also critical to identifying privacy violations and providing guidance for making the system inherently ethical. According to *Deloitte* (Eggers et al., 2020), in 2025, one of the government jobs will be algorithm auditor. Trained in technical skills such as data science, machine learning, and programming languages, algorithm auditors should have knowledge of ethics and fairness along with a practical understanding of how algorithms can affect citizens' daily lives. The work of algorithm auditors will consist of checking for black box issues, algorithmic bias and discrimination, identifying problems and providing recommendations for making the model more ethical and explainable. They will work with regulatory and judicial agencies to review algorithms and take preventive and corrective measures. Despite not being mentioned explicitly by Deloitte, algorithm auditors will also need social science skills, from social research methods and mixed quantitative and qualitative approaches to organisation analysis and from systematic comparison to case studies. As the need for algorithm auditors is growing, innovative forms of recognition outside organised education and training systems should be used to accredit these emerging skills, such as the Open Badges. The Open Badges are a method of accreditation adapted to the field of transversal skills of algorithm auditing, which are multiple complex skills that mobilise various forms of technical knowledge and associate different professions in the scientific and social fields.

Conclusions

Algorithms are not useful in and of themselves. It is what is undertaken with the algorithms that is important. The possibility of algorithms being unethical, independently of how ethics are conceived, is something that should be kept under control. Algorithms may challenge the entire ethical system, which has been created and institutionalised through information and communication technologies. The main reason is that, to face the guarantee of rights, it may be difficult to reconcile all the different ethical regulations and standard practices. What emerges is an "infraethic" (Floridi, 2014), a hyper-networked form of ethics in which the agents in the network may cause collateral consequences for all the others.

Nevertheless, because the actors who participate in algorithm assemblage are many and various (administrators and policymakers, politicians, business companies, researchers, journalists, and citizens), and they all have their own needs that may be partly in conflict, the balance between the needs of the different stakeholders should be managed politically. The politics of algorithms operates on at least three distinct levels: the disciplines, the stakeholders, and the administration of fairness. The importance of establishing a dialogue between different communities of experts is central to developing an algorithmic culture (Aragona, 2008) within algorithm assemblage. Furthermore, algorithms may alter the balance of power among different institutions and between the public/private and not-for-profit/ for-profit sectors. The issue of the difference between private actors, who are more concerned about consolidating their competitive advantage, and public actors, who aim to improve algorithmic transparency and accountability, is an interesting one. Furthermore, the provision of algorithmic literacy that teaches core concepts such as computational thinking, the role of data, and the importance of optimisation should be developed in education systems. This will increase citizens' and social groups' awareness of the data that they generate and the decisions that algorithms make using these data. The work of civil society is crucial in auditing algorithmic systems effectively. Through research and advocacy, often in cooperation with academia and journalists, it can intervene in policy debates around those systems, becoming a watchdog of algorithmic governance. There is, however, a need to train recognised professional figures who are able to unpack algorithmic assemblages and assess algorithms. Algorithm auditors may be crucial for shaping the future of our algorithmic societies and overcoming dystopic fears.

Conclusions

One of the main ways in which governance is being transformed through algorithmic systems is making it more technocratic in nature (Antonelli, 2019) and dependent on corporate interests that aim to subcontract many aspects of administrations' and citizens' lives. However, technological solutions on their own will not solve the problems unless they are contextualised, adaptable, and carefully targeted to achieve the objectives. Algorithms are means, not ends. Solutionism (Morozov, 2013), the idea that complex situations can be translated into precisely operationalised problems that can be solved or optimised through computation, is not sustained by facts. Technology cannot be seen as a way to tackle all problems of high expenditure, inefficiency, and human bias that have occurred, and will still certainly continue to occur, at all levels of public governance and in any field of policy. As noted, the expectations of intentional governance do not always fit into *de facto* governance (Voß and Kemp, 2006, pp. 8–9), which refers to the patterns and structures of the coordination of actions, the definition of problems, and the ways of approaching them that emerge from the interactions of many actors. A more sophisticated approach to automated decision systems and artificial intelligence should be firmly developed and adopted, taking into account the uniqueness of people, cultures, and places. It is fundamental for scholars to take an active role in researching algorithms through detailed empirical studies that can retrace the implications and consequences for the relevant stakeholders and envisage alternative socio-technical futures (Konrad and Böhle, 2019).

I introduced algorithm audit with the definition of auditing as it appears in the ISO, but in reality, there are not standardised audit experiences, carried out independently and through systematic procedures recognised by stakeholders. This is because, although exemplary studies urge governments to make their automated decision systems transparent, these are mainly experiences born in investigative journalism and academia. There are still no audit experiences, carried out by third parties, that express an independent assessment based on parameters defined and shared by all the stakeholders interested in the adoption of automated systems. As explained in Chapter 4, for the many examples presented in this book to form one step towards identifying methods and procedures for carrying out an algorithm audit, the institution of a public register of the algorithms employed in administrations is fundamental. The register will allow benchmarking, improving the quality of algorithmic systems, and avoiding the possibility that, after specific algorithms have been assessed as biased and unfair, they will still be employed in other policy or administrative contexts.

There are still no clear answers to the difficult questions raised by the increasing use of algorithms in public administrations, but the road to producing these answers is indicated and passes through a broad stakeholder engagement process, in which all stakeholders are equal, and through systematic and dedicated research. Politics should take action to establish the means by which this engagement has to happen, and academia should take action to research algorithmic assemblage from every possible scientific perspective (social, technical, ethical, organisational, political, etc.), knowing that it will always be difficult to disentangle all the different apparatuses of the assemblage that are really intertwined.

Unpacking the algorithm assemblages may be one way to increase the system's responsiveness and give politics a new source of legitimation instead of producing new forms of technocratic regimes. The analysis of algorithmic assemblages may also shed light on counter-power. It is true that rationalisation processes based on algorithms and big data are one of the key elements that support the dynamics of global power, but it is equally true that the scientific approach based on the same technologies can be turned into a great social force of progress and emancipation. According to Antonelli (2016), "the domain and its criticism, the ruling élites and protest movements have appealed to data" (p. 360), and I would add "to algorithms". Along with the expansive domain of instrumental rationality by governments and corporations, there is the possibility of emancipatory rationality through algorithms, as many cases of platform activism (e.g., Milan, 2017) have shown.

A paramount issue that will make the difference is funding. According to the *International Data Corporation*, one of the best global providers of ICT solutions, spending on artificial intelligence technologies is expected to increase by 33% in Europe and 28% in the

United States between 2020 and 2023. How much of this spending will be employed to develop procedures for impact assessment and standards for auditing algorithms? Probably, if any, it will be a very small amount. Instead, to make sure that algorithmic systems will exert a positive impact on our societies, all stakeholders should ask for sources of funding aimed at auditing algorithms to be made available, enabling participation by stakeholders who have so far been inadequately represented.

The main field for employing algorithms is bureaucracy (Visentin, 2018). However, shifting to algorithmic systems under budgetary pressure is no solution in itself: it requires not less governance but a different kind of governance, which should develop rules for the private sector. We are now very far from the primitive stage of automation, in which the dilemma was whether to be for or against automation. At this stage, the crucial question concerns the extent to which private algorithmic systems can be fair, unbiased, and accountable. We need to find feasible standards of excellence that can be chosen as benchmarks. Much research in the social sciences has just focused on the critique of automation and algorithmic systems, and this will not make any real difference to the ways in which those systems are implemented in the public sector. This brings us back to the primitive stage, and it is quite unrealistic to believe that we really can step out of automation. Instead, I believe that we, as social scientists, really need to step into automation. We should build on the critiques to develop a methods for evaluating algorithmic solutions that are co-created and shared by the broadest possible range of stakeholders. We should press the governments to implement these methods, and push that any automated systems used by a public administration should be made public by default. It is also through public authorities that we can really endorse the responsibility to make the ADMs deployed in public administration auditable.

Bibliography

Airoldi, M. (2020). Lo spettro dell'algoritmo e le scienze sociali. *Prospettive critiche su macchine intelligenti e automazione delle disuguaglianze. Polis*, *35*(1), 111–128.

Amaturo, E. and Aragona, B. (2012). *La costruzione delle documentazione empirica*. In Amaturo, E. (ed.), *Metodologia della ricerca sociale*. Turin: Utet.

Amoore, L. (2006). Biometric borders: Governing mobilities in the war on terror. *Political Geography*, *25*(3), 336–351.

Anderson, C. W. (2011, October 26). Notes Towards an Analysis of Computational Journalism. *HIIG Discussion Paper Series*, 2012-1.

Anderson, L. (2016). Analytic autoethnography. *Journal of Contemporary Ethnography*, *35*(4), 373–395.

Andrejevic, M. (2013). *Infoglut: How too much information is changing the way we think and know*. New York, NY: Routledge.

Angwin, J., Larson, J., Mattu, S. and Kirchner, L. (2016, 23 May). Machine bias. *ProPublica*. Available from www.propublica.org/article/machine-bias-risk-assessments-in-criminal-sentencing.

Antonelli, F. (2016). Ambivalence of official statistics: Some theoretical–methodological notes. *International Review of Sociology*, *26*(3), 354–366.

Antonelli, F. (2019). *Tecnocrazia e democrazia. L'egemonia al tempo della società digitale*. Rome: L'Asino d'oro.

Aragona, B. (2008). Una nuova cultura del dato. *Sociologia e Ricerca Sociale*, *XXIX*(87), 159–172.

Aragona, B. (2020). Sistemi di decisione algoritmica e disuguaglianze sociali: le evidenze della ricerca, il ruolo della politica. *La Rivista delle Politiche Sociali*, *2*(20), 213–226.

Aragona, B., Arvidsson, A. and Felaco, C. (2020). Introduction. Ethnography of algorithms. The cultural analysis of a sociotechnical construct. *Etnografia e ricerca qualitativa*, *3*(20), 335–349.

Aragona, B. and De Rosa, R. (2017). Unpacking big data in education. A research framework. *Statistics, Politics and Policy*, *8*(2), 123–137.

Aragona, B. and De Rosa, R. (2018). Policy making at the time of big data: Datascape, datasphere, data culture. *Sociologia Italiana*, *11*, 173–187.

Aragona, B. and Felaco, C. (2019). Big data from below. Researching data assemblages. *Tecnoscienza: Italian Journal of Science & Technology Studies*, *10*(1), 51–70.

Aragona, B., Felaco, C. and Marino, M. (2018). The politics of big data assemblages. *Partecipazione e conflitto*, *11*(2), 448–471.

Arnkil, R., Järvensivu, A., Koski, P. and Piirainen, T. (2010). *Exploring the quadruple helix*. Brussels: European Union.

Bailey, S., Pierides, D., Brisley, A., Weisshaar, C. and Blakeman, T. (2020). Dismembering organisation: The coordination of algorithmic work in healthcare. *Current Sociology*, *68*(4), 546–571.

Baltas, G. (2001). The effects of nutrition information on consumer choice. *Journal of Advertising Research*, *41*(2), 57–63.

Barsan, I. (2021) Quantifying the accuracy of vision/facial recognition on identifying PPE masks. Available from www.wundermanthompson.com/insight/ai-and-gender-bias.

Beer, D. (2013). *Popular culture and new media: The politics of circulation*, Basingstoke: Palgrave Macmillan.

Bengio, Y., Goodfellow, I. and Courville, A. (2017). *Deep learning*, Cambridge, MA: MIT Press.

Bergmann, U., Bonefeld-Dahl, C., Dignum, V., Gagné, J. F., Metzinger, T., Petit, N., Steinacker, S., Van Wynsberghe, A. and Yeung, K. (2019). *Ethics guidelines for trustworthy AI*. Brussels: European Union.

Berlinski, D. (2000). *The advent of the algorithm: The 300-year journey from an idea to the computer*, San Diego, CA: Harcourt.

Besley, T. and Hennessy, P. (2009, 17 June). *The global financial crisis –why didn't anybody notice?*, London: British Academy Forum. Available from wwwf.imperial.ac.uk/~bin06/M3A22/queen-lse.pdf)

Betancourt, M. (2017). *Glitch art in theory and practice: Critical failures and post-digital aesthetics*. Abingdon: Routledge.

Bourdieu, P. (1979). Symbolic power. *Critique of Anthropology*, *4*(13–14), 77–85.

Bourdieu, P. (1988). Social space and symbolic power. *Sociological Theory*, *7*(1), 14–25.

Bourdieu, P. (1991). *Language and symbolic power*. Harvard, MA: Harvard University Press.

Bowker, G. C. (2013). Data flakes: An afterword to *'Raw data' is an oxymoron*. In Gitelman, L. (ed.), *'Raw data' is an oxymoron* (pp. 167–171). Cambridge, MA: MIT Press.

Bowker, G. and Star, L. (1999). *Sorting things out: Classification and its consequences*. Cambridge, MA: MIT Press.

Britt-Gran, A. B., Booth, P. and Bucher, T. (2020). To be or not to be algorithm aware: A question of a new digital divide?, 9 March, 1-18. Available from www.tandfonline.com/doi/full/10.1080/1369118X.2020.1736124

Broussard, M. (2018). *Artificial unintelligence: How computers misunderstand the world*. Cambridge, MA: MIT Press.

Bucher, T. (2017). The algorithmic imaginary: Exploring the ordinary affects of Facebook algorithms. *Information, Communication & Society*, *20*(1), 30–44.

Bucher, T. (2018). *If …. then: Algorithmic power and politics*. New York, NY: Oxford University Press.

Burrell, J. (2015). How the machine 'Thinks:' Understanding opacity in machine learning algorithms. *Big Data & Society*, *3*(1), 1–12.

Caliandro, A. (2018). Digital methods for ethnography: Analytical concepts for ethnographers exploring social media environments. *Journal of Contemporary Ethnography*, *47*(5), 551–578.

Callon, M. and Law, J. (2005). On calculation, agency, and otherness. *Environment and Planning D: Society and Space*, *23*(5), 717–733.

Capra, F. (2021). Ecco l'errore che è costato la zona rossa alla Lombardia: Migliaia di guariti contati come positivi. *Fanpage*. Retrieved from www. fanpage.it/milano/ecco-lerrore-che-e-costato-la-zona-rossa-alla-lombardia-migliaia-di-guariti-contati-come-positivi/

Cheftel, J. C. (2005). Food and nutrition labelling in the European Union. *Food Chemistry*, *93*(3), 531–550.

Chignard, S. (2013). A brief history of open data. *Paris Tech Review*, 29 March. Retrieved from www.paristechreview.com/2013/03/29brief-history-open-data/

Chiusi, F., Fischer, S., Kayser-Bril, N. and Spielkamp, M. (2020). *Automating society report*. Berlin: Algorithm Watch.

Cicourel, A. V. (1995). *The social organization of juvenile justice* (Vol. 36). Livingston, NJ: Transaction Publishers.

Compaine, B. M. (2001). *The digital divide: Facing a crisis or creating a myth?* Cambridge, MA: MIT Press.

Cori, A., Ferguson, N. M., Fraser, C. and Cauchemez, S. (2013). A new framework and software to estimate time-varying reproduction numbers during epidemics. *American Journal of Epidemiology*, *178*(9), 1505–1512.

Dal Lago, A. and De Biasi, R. (2014) *Un certo sguardo: Introduzione all'etnografia sociale*. Bari: Laterza.

Davies, H. T., Nutley, S. M. and Walter, I. (2007). *Using evidence: How research can inform public services*. Bristol: Policy Press.

Davies, P. (2012). The state of evidence-based policy evaluation and its role in policy formation. *National Institute Economic Review*, *219*(1), 41–52.

Deleuze, G. and Guattari, F. (1980). *Mille Plateaux. Capitalisme et Schizophrénie*. Paris: Les Editions de Minuit.

Deriu, F. (2020). Luci e ombre dell'innovazione digitale nel welfare dei servizi alla persona in Italia. *La Rivista delle Politiche sociali*, *3*, 255–271.

Desrosières, A. (1998). *The politics of large numbers: A history of statistical reasoning*, Cambridge, MA: Harvard University Press.

Desrosières, A. (2010). *La politique des grands nombres*. Paris: Editions La Découverte.

Desrosières, A. and Thévenot, L. (1988). *Les catégories socioprofessionnelles*. Paris: Editions La Découverte.

Diakopoulos, N. (2016) Accountability in algorithmic decision making. *Communications of the ACM*, 59, 56–62.

Dieterich, W., Mendoza, C. and Brennan, T. (2016). *COMPAS risk scales: Demonstrating accuracy equity and predictive parity*. Traverse City, MI: Northpoint Inc.

Dourish, P. (2016). Algorithms and their others: Algorithmic culture in context. *Big Data & Society*, *3*(2), 1–11.

Eggers, W. D., Coltin, K. and Datar, A. (2020). *Government jobs of the future*. London: Deloitte. Available from www2.deloitte.com/content/dam/insights/us/articles/4767_FoW-in-govt/DI_Algorithm-auditor.pdf.

Espeland, W. N. and Stevens, M. L. (1998). Commensuration as a social process. *Annual Review of Sociology*, *24*(1), 313–343.

Espeland, W. N. and Yung, W. (2019). Ethical dimensions of quantification. *Social Science Information*, *58*(2), 238–260.

Eubanks, V. (2018). *Automating inequality: How high-tech tools profile, police, and punish the poor*. New York, NY: St. Martin's Press.

European Union (2020, 19 February). *Press remarks by President von der Leyen on the commission's new strategy: Shaping Europe's digital future*. Available from https://ec.europa.eu/commission/presscorner/detail/en/ac_20_260..

Eurostat (2009). *Standard quality report*. Luxembourg: Eurostat.

Fagan, M. E. (1976). Design and code inspections to reduce errors in program development. *IBM Systems Journal*, *15*(3), 182–211.

Feldman, M. S. and Pentland, B. T. (2008). Routine dynamics. In Barry, D. and Hansen, H. (eds.),*The Sage handbook of new approaches in management and organization* (pp. 302–315)). Los Angeles, CA: SAGE Publications.

Ferguson, A. G. (2017). *The rise of big data policing: Surveillance, race, and the future of law enforcement*. New York, NY: New York University Press.

Ferro, E., Loukis, E. N., Charalabidis, Y. and Osella, M. (2013). Policy making 2.0: From theory to practice. *Government Information Quarterly*, *30*(2013), 359–368.

Fisher, L. (1935). *The design of experiments*. Edinburgh: Oliever and Boyd.

Floridi, L. (2014). *The fourth revolution: How the infosphere is reshaping human reality*. Oxford: Oxford University Press.

Foucault, M. (1980). *Power/knowledge*. New York, NY: Pantheon Books.

Fowler, F. J. Jr and Mangione, T. W. (1990) *Standardized survey interviewing: Minimizing interviewer-related error* (Vol. 18). New York, NY: SAGE Publications.

Friedman, B. and Nissenbaum, H. (1996). Bias in computer systems. *ACM Transactions on Information Systems (TOIS)*, *14*(3), 330–347.

Geiger, R. S. (2017). Beyond opening up the black box: Investigating the role of algorithmic systems in Wikipedian organizational culture. *Big Data & Society*, *4*(2), 1–14.

Gillespie, T. (2014). The relevance of algorithms. In Gillespie, T., Boczkowski, P. and Foot, K. A. (eds.), *Media technologies: Essays on communication, materiality, and society* (pp. 167–194)). Cambridge, MA: MIT Press.

Gobo, G. (2008). *Doing ethnography*. New York, NY: SAGE Publications.

Goffey, A. (2008). Algorithm. In Fuller, M. (ed.), *Software studies – A lexicon* (pp. 15–20). Cambridge, MA: MIT Press.

Goldschlager, L. and Lister, A. (1986). *Computer science: A modern introduction*, London: Prentice Hall International.

Goodman, B. and Flaxman, S. (2017). European Union regulations on algorithmic decision-making and a 'right to explanation'. *AI Magazine, 38*(3), 26–30.

Gordon Legal. (2021). *Robodebt class action settlement* (accessed 23 February 2021), https://gordonlegal.com.au/robodebt-class-action/.

Greenwald, G., MacAskill, E. and Poitras, L. (2013, 11 June). Edward Snowden: The whistleblower behind the NSA surveillance revelations, *The Guardian.* (Accessible at www.theguardian.com/world/2013/jun/09/edward-snowden-nsa-whistleblower-surveillance)

Grønsund, T. and Aanestad, M. (2020). Augmenting the algorithm: Emerging human-in-the-loop work configurations. *The Journal of Strategic Information Systems, 29*(2), 101614.

Grosser, B. (2014). What do metrics want? How quantification prescribes social interaction on Facebook. *Computational Culture, 1*(4). http://computational-culture.net/what-do-metrics-want/.

Grudin, J. and Pruitt, J. (2002). Personas, participatory design and product development: An infrastructure for engagement. *Proceedings of Participatory Design Conference (PDC)*, vol. 2, 144–152.

Gurevich, Y. (2011). *What is an algorithm.* Redmond, WA: Microsoft Research.

Guszcza, J., Rahwan, I., Bible, W. and Cebrian, M. (2018). *Why we need to audit algorithms. Harvard Business Review.* 28 November. Available from https://hbr.org/2018/11/why-we-need-to-audit-algorithms

Hacking, I. (1982). Biopower and the avalanche of numbers. *Humanities in Society, 5*(3–4), 279–295.

Hacking, I. (2007). Kinds of people: Moving targets. In Marshall, P. J. (ed.), *Proceedings of the British Academy*, p. 285. doi:10.5871/bacad/9780197264249.003.0010.

Halford, S. and Savage, M. (2010). Reconceptualising digital social inequality. *Information, Communication and Society, 13*(7), 937–955.

Hallinan, B. and Striphas, T. (2016). Recommended for you: The Netflix Prize and the production of algorithmic culture. *New Media & Society, 18*(1), 117–137.

Haraway, D. (1997). *Modest–Witness@Second–Millennium. FemaleMan–Meets–OncoMouse: Feminism and technoscience*, New York, NY: Routledge.

He, X., Lau, E. H. Y., Wu, P., Deng, X., Wang, J., Hao, X. and Leung, G. L. (2020). Temporal dynamics in viral shedding and transmissibility of COVID-19. *Nature Medicine, 26*, 672–675.

High-Level Expert Group on Artificial Intelligence. (2019). *The ethics guidelines for trustworthy AI* (accessed 3 March 2019), https://reurl.cc/RdM1gG.

Hirshon, M. (2019, 17 September). *AI 50: America's most promising artificial intelligence companies.* Forbes. https://www.forbes.com/sites/jilliandonfro/2019/09/17/ai-50-americas-most-promising-artificial-intelligence-companies/?sh=782b6c0b565c

Höchtl, J., Parycek, P. and Schöllhammer, R. (2016). Big data in the policy cycle: Policy decision making in the digital era. *Journal of Organizational Computing and Electronic Commerce*, *26*(1), 147–169.

Hughes, E. C. (1970). The humble and the proud: The comparative study of occupations. *The Sociological Quarterly*, *9*(2), 147–156.

Hung, T. W. and Yen, C. P. (2020). On the person-based predictive policing of AI. *Ethics Information and Technology*. 1 June. Available from https://link. springer.com/article/10.1007/s10676-020-09539-x

Introna, L. D. (2016). Algorithms, governance, and governmentality: On governing academic writing. *Science, Technology, & Human Values*, *41*(1), 17–49.

Kaun, A. (2020). *Automating welfare: consequences of automated decision-making for democratic values*. EASST-4S virPrague 2020, Prague.

Kayser-Bril, N. (2020, 7 April). Google Apologizes after its Vision AI Produced Racist Results, *Algorithm Watch*. Available from https://algorithmwatch.org/ en/google-vision-racism/.

Kemper, J. and Kolkman, D. (2019). Transparent to whom? No algorithmic accountability without a critical audience. *Information, Communication & Society*, *22*(14), 2081–2096.

Kitchin, R. (2014). *The data revolution: Big data, open data, data infrastructures and their consequences*. London: SAGE Publications.

Kitchin, R. (2017). Thinking critically about and researching algorithms. *Information, Communication & Society*, *20*(1), 14–29.

Kitchin, R. and Lauriault, T. P. (2014). Towards critical data studies: Charting and unpacking data assemblages and their work. In Thatcher, J., Eckhert, J. and Shears, A. (eds.), *Thinking big data in geography: New regimes, new research* (Part 1). Lincoln, NA and London: University of Nebraska Press.

Kleinberg, J., Mullainathan, S. and Raghavan, M. (2016). Inherent trade-offs in the fair determination of risk scores. *Innovations in Theoretical Computer Science*, *67*(43), 1–23.

Knoblauch, H. (2005). Focused ethnography. *Forum: Qualitative Social Research*, *6*(3), 1–14.

Knorr-Cetina, K. (1999). *Epistemic cultures: How the sciences make knowledge*. Cambridge, MA: Harvard University Press.

Koene, A., Clifton, C., Hatada, Y., Webb, H. and Richardson, R. (2019). *A governance framework for algorithmic accountability and transparency*. Brussels: European Union.

Konrad, K. and Böhle, K. (2019). Socio-technical futures and the governance of innovation processes—An introduction to the special issue. *Futures*, *109*(2019), 101–107.

Kowalski, R. (1979). Algorithm = logic + control. *Communications of the Association for Computing Machinery*, *22*(7), 424–436.

Kushner, S. (2013). The freelance translation machine: Algorithmic culture and the invisible industry. *New Media & Society*, *15*(8), 1241–1258.

Landri, P. (2018). *Digital governance of education: Technology, standards and europeanization of education*, London: Bloomsbury.

Lane, J.-E. (2000). *New public management: An introduction.* New York, NY: Taylor & Francis.

Lasswell, H. D. (1951). The immediate future of research policy and method in political science. *American Political Science Review, 45*(March), 133–142.

Latour, B. (1987). *Science in action.* Cambridge, MA: Harvard University Press.

Lauriault, T. P. (2012). *Data, infrastructures and geographical imaginations* (Doctoral dissertation, Carleton University).

Lavrakas, P. J. (2008). *Encyclopedia of survey research methods* (Vols. 1-0). Thousand Oaks, CA: SAGE Publications.

Lenglet, M. (2011). Conflicting codes and codings: How algorithmic trading is reshaping financial regulation. *Theory, Culture & Society, 28*(6), 44–66.

Light, B., Burgess, J. and Duguay, S. (2018). The walkthrough method: An approach to the study of apps. *New Media & Society, 20*(3), 881–900.

Lupton, D. (2015). *Digital sociology.* Abingdon: Routledge.

Lyon, D. (2017). *Surveillance studies: An overview.* Cambridge: Polity Press.

MacKenzie, D. (2019). How algorithms interact: Goffman's 'interaction order' in automated trading. *Theory, Culture & Society, 36*(2), 39–59.

Milan, S. (2017). Data activism as the new frontier of media activism. In Yang, G. and Pickard, V. (eds.), *Media activism in the digital age* (pp. 130–152). Abingdon: Routledge.

Milano, S., Taddeo, M. and Floridi, L. (2020). Ethical aspects of multi-stakeholder recommendation systems. *The Information Society, 37*(1), 35–45.

Molnar, C. (2019) *Interpretable machine learning. A guide for making black box models explainable.* https://christophm.github.io/interpretable-ml-book/.

Morozov, E. (2013). *To save everything, click here: The folly of technological solutionism.* New York, NY: Public Affairs.

Mulry, M. H. (2008). Coverage error. *Encyclopedia of Survey Research Methods, 1*, 162–167.

Murero, M. (2020). Building artificial intelligence for digital health. A sociotech-med approach, and a few surveillance nightmares. *Etnografia e ricerca qualitativa, 3*, 374–388.

Musiani, F. (2013). Governance by algorithms. *Internet Policy Review, 2*(3), 67–89.

Nakamura, L. (2013). The socio-algorithmics of race: Sorting it out in jihad worlds. In Shoshana, M. and Kelly, G. (eds.), *The new media of surveillance* (pp. 159–162). Abingdon: Routledge.

Napoli, P. M. (2014). On automation in media industries: Integrating algorithmic media production into media industries scholarship. *Media Industries, 1*(1), 33–38.

Napolitano, D. (2020). Where is the voice of the machine?. An ethnography of artificial voice socio-technical networks. *Etnografia e ricerca qualitativa, 13*(3), 351–372.

Neyland, D. (2015). On organizing algorithms. *Theory, Culture & Society, 32*(1), 119–132.

Nguyen, H. L. Q. (2019). Are credit markets still local? Evidence from bank branch closings. *American Economic Journal: Applied Economics, 11*(1), 1–32.

Noble, S. (2018). *Algorithms of oppression: How search engines reinforce racism.* New York, NY: New York University Press.

Norris, P. (2001). *Digital divide: Civic engagement, information poverty and the internet worldwide.* Cambridge, MA: Cambridge University Press.

O'Neil, C. (2016). *Weapons of math destruction: How big data increases inequality and threatens democracy.* New York, NY: Crown Random House.

OECD (2015). *Exploring data-driven innovation as a new source of growth mapping the policy issues raised by "big data".* Paris: OECD.

OECD (2019). Data accessibility: Open, free and accessible formats, In *Government at a glance 2019*, Paris: OECD Publishing.

Pasquale, F. (2015). *The black box society: The secret algorithms that control money and information.* Cambridge, MA: Harvard University Press.

Persaud, J. (2020, 20 August). Home-educated children left abandoned in exams grade debacle, *The Telegraph.* Available from www.telegraph.co.uk/education-and-careers/2020/08/20/home-educated-children-left-abandoned-exams-grade-debacle/rgn=main;view=fulltext.

Quilty, B. J., Clifford, S., Hellewell, J., Russell, T. W., Kucharski, A. J., Flasche, S. and Davies, N. G. (2021). Quarantine and testing strategies in contact tracing for SARS-CoV-2: A modelling study. *The Lancet Public Health*, 6(3), e175–e183.

Reichenbach, H. (1938). *Experience and prediction. An analysis of the foundations and the structure of knowledge.* Chicago, IL: The University of Chicago Press.

Renzenbrink, L. (2020). *Interview with Cathy O'Neil*, In AA.VV. *Amsterdam intelligence*, Amsterdam: Colophon. Available from https://assets.amsterdam.nl/publish/pages/922120/amsterdam_intelligence.pdf.

Ribeiro, M. T., Singh, S. and Guestrin, C. (2016). *Model-agnostic interpretability of machine learning.* ICML Workshop on Human Interpretability in Machine Learning.

Ribes, D. and Jackson, S. J. (2013). Data bite man: The work of sustaining long-term study. In Gitelman, L. (ed.), *'Raw data' is an oxymoron* (pp. 147–166). Cambridge, MA: MIT Press.

Rogers, R. (2013). *Digital methods.* Cambridge, MA: MIT Press.

Rovatsos, M., Mittelstadt, B. and Koene, A. (2020). *Bias in algorithmic decision-making.* London: Centre for Data Ethics and Innovation (CDEI).

Ruppert, E., Harvey, P., Lury, C., Mackenzie, A., McNally, R., Baker, S. A. and Lewis, C. (2015). Socialising big data: From concept to practice. *CRESC Working Paper Series 138.* Retrieved from http://hummedia.manchester.ac.uk/institutes/cresc/workingpapers/wp138.pdf

Ruppert, E., Isin, E. and Bigo, D. (2017). Data politics. *Big Data & Society*, 4(2), 1–7.

Sagiroglu, S. and Sinanc, D. (2013). Big data: A review. In *Collaboration technologies and systems (CTS), 2013 international conference CTS 20–24* (pp. 42–47). May San Diego: IEEE.

Salais, R. (2004). La politique des indicateurs. Du taux de chômage au taux d'emploi dans la stratégie européenne pour l'emploi (SEE). In Zimmermann, B. (ed.), *Action publique et sciences sociales* (pp. 311–325). Paris: Editions de la Maison des Sciences de l'Homme.

Salais, R. and Storper, M. (1993). Les mondes de production (enquête sur l'identité économique de la France). *Genèses, Sciences sociales et histoire, 20,* 170–171.

Salganik, M. J. (2018). *Bit by bit: Social research in the digital age.* Princeton, NJ: Princeton Press.

Salganik, M. J. and Levy, K. E. (2015). Wiki surveys: Open and quantifiable social data collection. *PloS One, 10*(5), 23–48.

Salvucci, A., Giorgi, M., Barchiesi, E. and Scafidi, M. (2017). *Perizia tecnica preliminare sull'analisi dell'algoritmo che gestisce il software della mobilità docenti per l'a.s. 2016/2017.* Available from www.gildavenezia.it/wp-content/uploads/2017/06/Perizia-tecnica-preliminare2017.pdf

Seaver, N. (2013) Knowing algorithms. *Media in Transition, 8,* 1–12.

Seaver, N. (2018). What should an anthropology of algorithms do? *Cultural Anthropology, 33*(3), 375–385.

Sen, A. (1990). Justice: Means versus freedoms. *Philosophy and Public Affairs, 19*(2), 111–121.

Sen, A. (1993). Positional objectivity. *Philosophy and Public Affairs, 22*(2), 126–145.

Senate Community Affairs Committee Secretariat (2017). *Design, scope, cost-benefit analysis, contracts awarded and implementation associated with the better management of the social welfare system initiative.* Canberra: Australian Ministry of Community Affairs.

Shokri, R. and Shmatikov, V. (2015). Privacy-preserving deep learning. In *Proceedings of the 22nd ACM SIGSAC conference on computer and communications security* (pp. 1310–1321).

Sipser, M. (2006). *Introduction to the theory of computation.* Boston, MA: Thompson Learning.

Skirpan, M. and Gorelick, M. (2017). The authority of "fair" in machine learning. *arXiv preprint arXiv:1706.09976.*

Smith, A. (2018) *Reconceptualising happiness with the Geluksmeter: how algorithms shape norms and values relating to happiness.* Presentation at the conference Human-Technology Relations: Postphenomenology and Philosophy of Technology, University of Twente (NL), 9 July 2018.

Smith, M. (2016). *Deloitte: Automation Set to Transform Public Services.* Deloitte press. 25 October. Available from www2.deloitte.com/uk/en/pages/press-releases/articles/automation-set-to-transform-public-services.html.

Star, S. L. (1999). The ethnography of infrastructure. *American Behavioral Scientist, 43*(3), 377–391.

Stewart, F. (2014). Against happiness: A critical appraisal of the use of measures of happiness for evaluating progress in development. *Journal of Human Development and Capabilities, 15*(4), 293–307.

Takhteyev, Y. (2012). *Coding places: Software practice in a South American City.* Cambridge, MA: MIT Press.

Tene, O. and Polonetsky, J. (2012). Big data for all: Privacy and user control in the age of analytics. *Northwestern Journal of Technology and Intellectual Property, 11*(5), 239–273.

Thévenot, L. (1984). Rules and implements: Investment in forms. *Social science information*, *23*(1), 1–45.

Torenholt, R. and Langstrup, H. (2021) Between a logic of disruption and a logic of continuation: Negotiating the legitimacy of algorithms used in automated clinical decision-making. *Health*. doi:10.1177/1363459321996741.

Trivellato, U. (2002). Qualità dell'informazione statistica ufficiale e esigenze informative di regioni e città. In *Relazione presentata alla VI Conferenza nazionale di Statistica* (pp. 6–8).

Uchida, C. (2014). Predictive policing. In Bruinsma, G. and Weisburd, D. (eds.), *Encyclopedia of criminology and criminal justice* (pp. 3871–3880). Cham: Springer International.

United Nations (2018) About the sustainable development goals. Available from www.un.org/sustainabledevelopment/sustainable-development-goals

Van Couvering, E. (2007). Is relevance relevant? Market, science, and war: Discourses of search writing. *Science, Technology, & Human Values*, *41*(1), 17–49.

van den Ord, A., Dieleman, S., Zen, H., Simonyan, K., Vinyals, O., Graves, A., Kalchbrenner, N., Senior, A. W. and Kavukcuoglu, K. (2016). WaveNet: A Generative Model for Raw Audio, arXiv:1609.03499.

van Dijk, J. (2020). *The digital divide*. Cambridge: Polity Press.

Verdacht, B. V. (2021). *SyRI-coalitie aan Eerste Kamer: 'Super SyRI' blauwdruk voor meer toeslagenaffaires*. Retrieved from: https://platformburgerrechten.nl/2021/01/11/syri-coalitie-aan-eerste-kamer-super-syri-blauwdruk-voor-meer-toeslagenaffaires/.

Vervloesem, K. (2020). How Dutch activists got an invasive fraud detection algorithm banned. In Chiusi, F., Fischer, S., Kayser-Bril, N. and Spielkamp, M. (eds.), *Automating society report 2020* (pp. 160–163). Berlin: AlgorithmWatch gGmbH.

Visentin, C. (2018). Il potere razionale degli algoritmi tra burocrazie e nuovi idealtipi. *The Lab's Quarterly*, *20*(3), 47–72.

Voorberg, W. H., Bekkers, V. J. and Tummers, L. G. (2015). A systematic review of co-creation and co-production: Embarking on the social innovation journey. *Public Management Review*, *17*(9), 1333–1357.

Voß, J. P. and Kemp, R. (2006). Sustainability and reflexive governance: An introduction. In Voß, J.-P., Bauknecht, D. and Kemp, R. (eds.), *Reflexive governance for sustainable development* (pp. 3–28). Cheltenham: Edward Elgar.

Webb, E. J., Campbell, D. T., Schwartz, R. D. and Sechrest, L. (1966). *Unobtrusive measures: Non-reactive research in the social sciences*, Chicago, IL: Rand McNally.

Whelan, A. (2020). "Ask for more time": Big data chronopolitics in the Australian welfare bureaucracy. *Critical Sociology*, *46*(6), 867–880.

Williamson, B. (2016). Digital education governance: An introduction. *European Educational Research Journal*, *15*(1), 1–3.

Wong, P. H. (2020). Democratizing algorithmic fairness. *Philosophy and Technology*, *33*, 225–244.

Yeung, K. (2018). *Big data-driven government: Towards a new public analytics in public administration? Paper presented at the conference Identity, Security, Democracy: Challenges for Public Law*, Hong Kong University, 27/6/2018.

Yeung, K. and Lodge, M. (2019). *Algorithmic regulation*. Oxford: Oxford University Press.

Zunino, C. (2019, 17 September). Scuola, trasferimenti di 10mila docenti lontano da casa. Il Tar: "L'algoritmo impazzito fu contro la Costituzione", *La Repubblica*. Available from www.repubblica.it/cronaca/2019/09/17/news/scuola_trasferimenti_di_10mila_docenti_lonta   no_da_casa_il_tar_l_algoritmo_impazzito_fu_contro_la_costituzione_-236215790/.

Index

access 48; to algorithm assemblage 34; to data 23–24; to technology 9
accountability xvii–xviii, 50, 53; of public bodies 10–11, 52
accuracy 20; of Google Vision API 36
agent 3, 13, 57; AI-powered 52
algocracy 46
algorithm xi; audit *see* audit; awareness *see* awareness, algorithmic; deterministic xiii; recipe xviii; success 24
algorithmic: decision system *see* automated decision system; impact assessment 29, 30; readiness 56
Amaturo, E. 33, 62
Amsterdam 14, 28, 31, 69
analytics 29–30
ANPR 37–38
anti-classification 27
API 36
Artificial Intelligence (AI) 52; human AI 13; trustworthy AI 17, 50–51
assemblage xv–xvi, 3; algorithm 34
assessment 46; impact 29–30, 55; of fairness xviii
audit 16–17; algorithm xvii, 18, 47, 56; models 24–25
auditor 16, 48, 57
automated decision system (ADS) xiv, 39, 50, 59

automation 50, 52, 61; impact of 29
awareness xviii, 12, 46, 48, 56; algorithmic 12, 55; passive 55; of the data 58
Azure 37

Barsan, I. 36–37, 39
batch 21
Beer, D. xv, 63
bias xx, 19, 28, 37, 54; cultural 36; human 59; selection 18
big data xx–xxi
biometric 53
black box xvi, xix, 4–7, 17, 35
Bourdieu, P. 2
Broussard, M. 9, 30
Bucher, T. xii, xviii, 7

calibration 27
co-creation 47–48; quadruple helix 55
coding 20; team 40
comparability 20–22
compass 18–19, 23, 27
computational xii, 3
counter-power 60
coverage errors 20
COVID-19 ix, xiv, 20, 22
crime xvi, 18–19, 25
critical algorithm studies xiv–xv, 3
crowdsourcing 45
culture xiv–xv, 39–40; algorithmic culture 9, 56, 58

For Product Safety Concerns and Information please contact our EU
representative GPSR@taylorandfrancis.com
Taylor & Francis Verlag GmbH, Kaufingerstraße 24, 80331 München, Germany